Talents

Story by

Kenyata Martin

Kenyata Martin

ISBN-978-0-692-14820-4

Chapter One

By the time I met my father I was seven years old. I still remember that day. I recall constantly peeping through the blinds and being stunned when I saw his car roll up in the driveway. I was excited that he had truly made good on his promise, for once. He took me over to his parents' house, leaving me there for several hours. He then came back and picked me up, returning me back to my mother.

That was all.

Spending time with him during the forty-minute drive to and from my mother's house was still an amazing time for me. It would be years before I ever physically saw him again. And when I did see him again, he would be in prison.

My dad was a local celebrity of sorts. He played multiple instruments in the church band. He was exceptional with his skill set, so he would often travel to different churches throughout our small city. Because of his popularity and travels, he became popular with the ladies. My dad was tall with dark skin; he was strikingly handsome with a dazzling smile. He wore his shoulder length hair straight, and he always dressed in posh suits. Because of his musical ingenuity, the ladies flocked to him.

The fact that my dad was in the church meant nothing as far as lifestyle goes. When he wasn't rocking the piano on the pew, he was in

4

the streets selling cocaine. He wasn't as good at selling drugs as he was at playing the piano though. He kept getting caught. Subsequently, he was in prison more than he was in the church.

It was my grandfather who raised me. My mother's father was someone to be admired. He was retired from the military, and he went on to make a career as a head janitor for the military. He was also the lead deacon in our church. He and my grandmother owned a quaint four-bedroom ranch house in Tifton, GA. Tifton is just one hundred and eighty two miles south of Atlanta, population just a little over fifteen thousand people. It's a small town, decorated with pine trees and a vast grassy landscape. It is a major distribution hub for the southeast corridor and home to the beginning of what we now know as an interstate.

Not long after my mother left my father, she fell in love with another smooth talker named Ralph. My grandparents didn't approve of this new relationship. The rumor was that he was violent. My grandparents never had anything good to say about him. I used to stand near the doorway of my room and listen as my grandparents pleaded with my mom to leave him. I had never seen my mother abused, but Ralph was intimidating in size. He was tall and hulking, and he liked to lift weights. He was daunting in size alone. If he grew angry enough, the threat of his rage alone would be considered abuse.

No matter how much my grandparents protested, they couldn't convince my mother to leave Ralph. As a compromise, everyone agreed

5

that it would be in my two older sisters' and my best interest if we lived with them. Meanwhile, my mother went on to start her life with her new man.

My mom didn't go far though. Right behind my grandparents' home, in the backyard, was a small, white church. This was not the church we attended but a church all the same. Right beyond that church, half a football field's distance away, was where my mother and her boyfriend lived. I only had to walk five minutes to get to her home. If I ran I could get there in two.

My grandparents were old school; they believed in church and discipline. I mean old school like, "Go and pick your own switch to get spanked with," old school. As bad as I was, I can honestly tell you there is no way to properly pick a switch that will work in your favor. Between getting spanked and being in church every day, one would think the discipline would have kept me on the straight and narrow. It didn't.

I grew up with my two cousins, Germ and Brian. We were in the same age group, so we had a lot of the same interests. We were infamous for sneaking out of church service, and we all loved playing football. Germ and Brian were at my grandfather's house all the time. We spent a lot of time trolling the neighborhood looking for something to get into. If we weren't doing chores around the house for our grandfather, we were at the park playing football or basketball.

Football was my first love, and I was good at it. My cousins and I used to compete fiercely with one another about most things, and we would even throw hands if it came to that. Those instances were far and few between, but that's how I learned how to fight. Knowing how to fight was a necessary evil growing up in Tifton. We used to play football across the tracks in our rival school's neighborhood, and almost every time the game would end in an all-out fist fight.

My cousin Brian and I were the closest. It was because of him that I learned how to drive when I was only eight years old. My mom owned a Ford Escort. It was brand new with a fresh red paint job and shiny chrome wheels. That was a popular car in those days, Brian and I were obsessed with it. I would usually stay at my mom's house on the weekends. On these days, Brian and I would beg my mom to let us wash her car, just so she would give us the keys. My mom was an avid wrestling fan. Once wrestling came on the television, we knew she would be preoccupied until all the matches were done.

Being that she worked two jobs, she would usually fall asleep before the program ended. This is when we would have the car keys. True to our word, we would always wash the car, but the other three hours were spent joy riding. I even taught myself how to drive. I had watched and studied others while they drove. From there, I basically followed the steps. With Brian egging me on, I was driving as well as any twenty-year-old in just three months' time.

While my cousins were around most days, Warren was over the house every day for real. Warren was my best friend and we had each other's backs. We threw hands with the best of them. We would scuffle in any neighborhood about anything and run all the way home laughing.

Then, one day, everything that I knew to be consistent changed. It began in the evening while I was at home sitting on the couch watching television. Without warning, I heard someone on the front porch banging on my grandparents' screen door. I darted to the screen door, and it was Warren.

"Hurry up, let's go to the park, the police up there!" he yelled excitedly.

I didn't ask any questions, I just threw on my sneakers and ran up to the park with him. I knew it had to be something outrageous happening if the police were there. We ran up the street towards the park; the blue lights were throbbing in the sky, beckoning us from a block away. It was dusk when we got to the park and, true to Warren's word, it was teeming with police. Warren started asking spectators what had happened. Turns out, someone had gotten his head busted open with a baseball bat during a fight and had died on the scene! This was the first time I had even considered what death was, and by the time we had gotten there, the body was already gone. The feeling of loss and violence tainted the feeling of community, even after the body had long been carted away.

That night, I stayed up late, tossing and turning in my bed. Though I hadn't seen a body, and didn't know the persons involved, my brain repeatedly imagined what had happened. I thought about it so much that I couldn't sleep. I kept imagining the victim, lying on the ground with blood leaking from his skull, a bloody baseball bat lying nearby, his eyes staring off into nothingness.

As I lay awake staring at the ceiling, still reliving the murder at the park, my oldest sister suddenly appeared in the doorway.

"What?" I shouted, almost screaming.

She had scared me. It was three in the morning. I assumed that she had heard me tossing and turning and knew that I was disturbed. I thought she had shown up to be a big sister and to console me.

"Pack your clothes," she said flatly.

"For what?" I asked, sitting up.

She walked over and sat down on the edge of the bed. "We're moving to Atlanta."

I was puzzled. "When? Tonight? Where's Mama?"

She held her index finger up to the tip of her nose. "Sh. Just do it, and be quiet."

She mushed me in the face softly, and my head fell back into the pillows.

I lay in silence for a moment. I didn't believe her, but when she was gone, I could hear her and my other sister fumbling around in her room.

My grandmother showed up moments later. I threw my legs over

9

the side of the bed, letting my feet rest on the wooden floor. She held her robe snug against her chest as she crossed the floor and sat down on the bed next to me. "What Pamela talking about, Grandma?" I asked, confused.

"Who we moving to Atlanta with?"

"Don't worry, baby."

She pulled me close and hugged me.

"Your momma is coming to get you and take you to Atlanta with her. She wants all her kids to be together." She began to rock slightly as she held me. "Lord knows, it's the best thing for yawl," she mumbled under her breath.

She let me go, and I walked over to my closet and pulled out my suitcase as my grandmother left the room. I sat the suitcase on top of the bed. I thought about having to leave my cousins. I thought about leaving my best friend Warren. I couldn't help but wonder if the murder at the park was the reason why my mom wanted to take us away from Tifton. Begrudgingly, I packed.

I packed with only the light from the hallway filling the room. I didn't put the room light on because there was a sense of suspicion in the air. I felt like we were sneaking. The fuller my suitcase became the more upset I became with the idea of leaving. All my friends were in Tifton. It was all I knew. I had spent the first nine years of my life there. When I was finally done with the packing, I sat my suitcase by the front door next to my sisters' suitcases. I got dressed and lay back in my bed and waited. At 5:30 am, my grandfather came to my bedroom door.

"Get up, boy, and help me put these suitcases in your Mama's car," he said firmly.

I quickly got up and met him at the front door. My mother's car was parked outside in the driveway. I took my suitcase outside and followed after my grandfather, who was carrying my sisters' two suitcases. My mother was sitting in the driver's seat. I stopped at the driver's side and she let the window down.

"Momma, why we moving to Atlanta?" I asked.

She smiled big. "I found a new place, baby. Don't you want to live in a new place? See new things? Meet new people?"

I nodded, yes. It was then that I saw the chrome .380 handgun resting openly in her lap. It was still dark outside, and the chrome glimmered in the moonlight.

"Where is Ralph?" I asked, quickly shifting my gaze.

"He's at work," she said, not offering any more information.

Something told me that if he did show up, a problem would ensue in a matter of seconds.

My grandfather swatted me lightly across the back of the head.

"Put that bag in the car, boy," he said, snatching me from my daydream.

The Ford Escort was filled with luggage. This wasn't an ordinary move; this was an escape. A short while later, we all five piled into the small car, my two older sisters and my younger brother and sister. They were the siblings my mom had given birth to while with Ralph.

We left Tifton, GA, that morning, just as the sun began to rise. We rode the two-hour journey to Atlanta in silence, mostly sleeping. I dreamt about the dead body at the park. I dreamt that it was my mother who had killed someone at the park. I dreamed all the way to Atlanta.

When I woke up, we were pulling into our new apartment complex. We had made it to Atlanta. It smelled different; the air wasn't as vibrant, and the sky wasn't as broad. As I unloaded the suitcases I scanned the neighborhood as far as my eyes could see. I quickly resolved that I was going to miss Tifton.

Chapter Two

Atlanta was different. The city was bursting with skyscrapers, buildings taller than any of the buildings I had grown up around in Tifton. There were more people. We lived in the city of Lawrenceville, a small city twenty miles outside of Atlanta. The apartment we lived in was nice. It had stainless steel appliances, plush carpet, and fresh paint on the walls. It even had a dishwasher. There were a pool and basketball court in the complex. The only downside was that it was a two-bedroom apartment, and there were six of us. My sisters shared a room, my mother had her room, and my little brother and I were left to fend for ourselves. We crashed on the couch or just camped on the floor.

I quickly settled into a routine. I used to sit outside on the steps of our apartment building's breezeway. There were always kids outside, but I didn't know any of them. I figured that when I began school, I would meet new friends. At least that's what my mother told me. I thought about Warren and my cousins daily.

My mother knew I was homesick, so she called Uncle Lennie. She felt like I needed a male figure in my life. When I met up with Uncle Lennie, he asked me something that uplifted me.

"When was the last time you played football, Ken?" he asked.

He drove me to the local recreation center that same day and signed me up for intramural football.

Two weeks later, I was at practice with my new team. Up until this point, I had only played football at the local parks for recreation. Now I was playing organized football, and I was more than grateful for the opportunity and the challenge. After I joined the team, I began to meet new friends. Just like that, I soon began to forget about Tifton too.

I would practice football in my apartment complex. There were a couple of kids from the team who stayed in my neighborhood. Most of us had a lot in common, and football was the sport that kept us occupied. I had yet to build a close alliance with anyone. There was no one I considered a friend like Warren had been. I had come close to blows with other kids once or twice, but it never had to get physical.

I was cool with most of the other kids in my neighborhood, until I met Josh. I had seen and been around him since I first moved to the complex, but we had nothing in common. He was from New York, so he sounded different. He spoke proper, and it came off as if he thought he was better than everyone else. I decided to keep my distance.

One day we clashed. We were sitting on the picnic tables in the park at the back of the complex. We were arguing about rap music, and tensions were high. In those days, the south was just beginning to rise as a hip-hop force, and New York rappers were only then beginning to decline as the dominant entity in the rap game. Of course, Josh, being from New York, had a strong opinion about New York rappers whereas I myself cared nothing about New York or its rappers. We both had

14

strong opinions about this and, ultimately, we came to blows. We scuffled for a few quick seconds before our friends broke us up from fighting. This was the first fight that I had been in since I had left Tifton. This fight was different because it was the first time I had fought about something outside of football or territory. This was a fight about a difference of opinion and environment. I didn't walk away with the same feelings as I had about the other fights that I had been in prior to that day.

The next day, Josh and I saw each other at the park, and our friends brought us together to squash the beef. We all lived in the same neighborhood, and it was agreed that we should be united and protect our neighborhoods from others. Josh and I agreed that we would be stronger as a neighborhood if we all got along. From that day forward, we were tighter with each other than with most others.

Just as soon as our alliance was formed it ended abruptly. I came home from school one day and found that everything in our apartment was packed. In just three months' time, we were moving again.

"Why are we moving, Mama?" I asked, standing in her bathroom door.

She was loading toiletries into a box. "We need a bigger place. The girls need more room and privacy. Wouldn't you like to have your own room?"

I did want my own room, but I didn't want to leave my football

15

team or my new friends. "Are we moving back to Tifton?" I asked.

"No, we're not moving far from here." She folded the box shut and shoved it into my arms. "Take that to the car for me."

Later that evening, we loaded up the car and moved to the projects.

The projects were only ten minutes from our old place. But no sooner had we pulled onto the property than the difference in the neighborhood became immediately clear to us. The presence of more black people was obvious. They stood out on their stoops, watching as we pulled up to our new home. Groups of teenagers loitered near and on cars parked in the lot. The dumpster was littered with broken furniture and mattresses surrounding it.

I was slightly nervous as I got out the car and followed my mother up to our new apartment door. She opened the door and, true to her word, it was bigger. We had four bedrooms now but no dishwasher. Inside, my brother, sisters and I ran around the empty apartment claiming rooms and somersaulting in the open space.

Uncle Lennie and his friends unloaded the moving truck, and I helped them. Every time I went outside to grab a box, I would eye the neighborhood. The later the evening grew the more people began to hang out in breezeways and the parking lot. They clustered in groups of twos and threes.

Every car that turned onto the property had oversized wheels and heavy bass music blaring from the speakers. I was in love with my mother's Escort, but here I was falling in love with every other car that turned onto the property. I thought about my cousin Brian. I wished he was here to see all the cars I was seeing. I walked towards my building with a box filled with my things. My football helmet was on top of the box. A kid about my age rolled up on me on his bicycle before I made it to the corridor.

"What up?" he asked.

I nodded. "What's up?"

"You play football?"

"Yeah, do you?" I asked.

"That's why I asked," he said snidely.

"We have a football game tomorrow at the field. If you can play, show up tomorrow at one."

"Where's the field?" I asked.

He pointed to the rear of the projects. There was only a dark space as far as I could see. That was when I noticed a group of teenagers hanging off to the side of an adjacent building. I saw an older man walk up to the group before one of the guys went into his pocket and pulled out a handful of small baggies. The older man picked some of the baggies and handed the younger man a fold of money. I didn't know exactly what had taken place, but I did know that they were trying not

17

to be seen. That much was obvious.

"Well, you gonna show up or not?" the boy on the bike asked.

"Yeah, I'll be there."

"Cool, and, oh, you won't need that helmet," he said before riding off.

I watched him ride off, and then my eyes drifted back to the group of teenagers. They were standing around talking and smoking. I could smell what they were smoking, and it didn't smell like any cigarette or cigar I had ever smelt. I was intrigued. I was more interested in what they had going on than the football game the next day.

"Kenyatta! Get your ass in here!" I heard my mom call from the apartment door.

I headed inside.

I was nervous about the football game. Not because I thought that anyone was better than me but because usually when I played with a bunch of guys I didn't know Warren, Brian or Germ would have been with me. I still had my hand game to rely on though. At one o' clock, the grassy field behind the projects was active with kids and several teenagers. They were tossing the football back and forth, while the two captains were picking their teams. The two captains were older, they were in their late teens. As soon as I walked up, one of the captains said, "I got him," and pointed at me.

I didn't know why he picked me out of all the talent on the grass at that exact moment. I didn't have time to ponder much before my team captain called all his players into a huddle. He held the football tightly in his right hand. He was the captain and the quarterback. He had dark skin and was lanky with a short, wavy haircut. He wasn't dressed to play football. His watch was gold, and he had on three gold rings and a heavy gold chain. His crisp new Jordan sneakers were for show.

"What position you play, lil homey?" he asked me.

"Running back," I said bravely.

"I'm handing it to you," he said before breaking the huddle.

The captain/quarterback for the other team had on just as much jewelry as my captain. He was in his late teens as well. He only wore an A-frame T-shirt. He had cornrows and tattoos that covered his entire right arm. As I lined up, I realized that this football game was captain vs. captain. The kids my age were just pawns in this chess game.

"Hike!"

Immediately, the ball was shoved in my gut. The opposing team rushed. I faked left and spun right towards the sideline. Then I blew past the last defender for the touchdown.

"I told you! I told you!" the captain of my team exclaimed as he ran over to his nemesis and got in his face.

"Good run, homey," I heard someone say in my ear. I turned to see

19

the kid who was on the bike from the day before. He was on the other team.

He ran back down to his side of the field to receive the kick.

The quarterback for my team lined up with me.

"Good fucking run, Lil homey. I got something for you when the game over."

My team punted the ball.

We won the game by thirteen points. The quarterback for the losing team handed my quarterback a stack of money. And, true to his word, the quarterback of my team did have something for me. He peeled me off a twenty dollar bill from his bankroll.

"What's your name, lil homey?" he asked me.

"Ken," I said.

"They call me 'L,' Ken. Good game," he said before he walked off.

After the game, I was headed home when the guy on the bike rolled up on me; he rode beside me while I walked. "What's your name, bro?" he asked.

"They call me Ken," I replied.

Then, for the first time, I paid attention to the bike he was riding. It was a shiny chrome BMX with white mag wheels and pegs on the front and back.

"What's your name?"

"I'm Brad. Where you from?"

"I'm from Tifton, but I just moved here from Lawrenceville."

While we talked, two others rolled up on bikes almost identical to the one Brad had. One of the riders was a chubby black kid, and the other rider was a lanky white kid. They both appeared to be my age.

"These are my homies, Big Mark and Stan," Brad said, introducing the two other riders.

I nodded to both. Whereas Stan appeared to be cool, Big Mark had a hard edge about him.

"Nigga, let's go," Mark said, irritated, only glancing at me menacingly.

"You ain't got no bike?" Brad asked as if he had just read my mind.

"Nah," I replied.

Big Mark and Stan rode off down the street.

"We going to get you one tomorrow," Brad said as he sped off to catch up with the others.

Chapter Three

The next day, I hurried outside almost as soon as I woke up. There was more to see and do here in the projects than anywhere else that I had ever lived. I was making friends fast and seeing things I had never seen before in my life. I came out my apartment and walked around the neighborhood looking for Brad. I had spent most of the previous evening pondering what he had meant when he said he would get me a bike. I needed a bike. I knew I couldn't hang out with Brad and his crew if I didn't have one. I literally wouldn't be able to keep up with them.

I found a bench near the park and waited. I was only on the bench a few seconds before I heard Brad call my name. He rolled up on his bike quick.

"Hop on," he said.

I stepped onto the pegs attached to the rear wheels of his bike and held onto his shoulders as he took off.

"Where we headed?" I asked as he maneuvered through the neighborhood.

"We going to get you a bike," he said flatly.

We left the projects and rode through various neighborhoods. After about ten minutes of riding, the scenery began to change. The neighborhood became more affluent, and the houses that made up the area were big and expensive, three-leveled homes with spacious lawns and wide driveways.

"Start looking for your bike," Brad said.

At first, I didn't know what he meant, but I realized fast. As we rode past houses, I noticed many bikes in the driveways, on the porches or just lying in the yards unsecured. After about two blocks, I spotted a red BMX Diamond Back with black mag wheels lying up against a garage door.

"I see it," I said, pointing at the garage door where the bike lay.

"Man, don't point at the house!" Brad exclaimed. "You trying to go to jail."

He pulled up and stopped near a patch of woods only a few feet away from where I had seen the bike.

"Go get your bike," he told me.

I jumped off the back of the bike and looked up and down the street covertly. It looked like no one was home, there wasn't a car in the driveway. I was nervous, but I had come too far to turn back. I walked casually across the lawn and up the driveway. I hopped on the bike and sped away in a matter of seconds. Brad sped past me, and I followed him back to our neighborhood. We made it back to the projects without incident and in record time. Just like that, I had a new bike. I spent the better part of the day riding around to other apartment complexes with

Brad, Big Mark, and Stan. I was getting to know them. Stan was a white dude who grew up around black people, he was cool. Brad was the pretty boy, always brushing the waves in his hair and meticulously dressing the part. Big Mark was the muscle. He was heavy set with a menacing scowl. Although he was overweight, it was clear that the average kid our age wouldn't want to rumble with him.

It didn't take long for the three of us to become the best of friends. I was accepted into the group almost immediately. I'm sure it was because I was willing to participate in any activity that the group introduced. It became routine for us to steal bikes; then we graduated from that and started to break into houses. We would skip school, go to the more prosperous neighborhoods, and break into homes while the owners were at work. It seemed that no sooner had I had moved to the projects than I began a life of crime.

My criminal career advanced as the next several months passed. Before I knew it, criminal activity had become a way of life. Once Brad and the others learned that I could drive, it wasn't long before we were stealing cars. Brad had learned how to pop the lock box at the car dealerships. This allowed us keys to every new car parked on a dealer's lot. We ditched the bikes, and now we were cruising the entire city in new cars. Now, when we broke into houses, we could steal more in one setting, which meant we had more stuff to sell.

It wasn't long after we started stealing cars that we began to venture further outside of our city limits. We used to visit girls from other schools, go to football games at other schools, and buy a better grade of weed than we could get in our own neighborhood. Stan was the one who introduced us to marijuana. He used to steal it from his dad's stash. It was Big Mark who found out where we could buy our own weed. One day, we took a trip to Decatur, GA. It is a city about ten miles away from our projects. I was the best driver of us all, so I always drove when we rode out for a long distance.

"What's the name of the apartments again?" I asked as we cruised down Interstate 85 headed south.

"East Hampton," Mark said from the rear seat.

Brad was up front in the passenger's seat.

"You ain't never heard of the 'Hamp'?" Brad asked.

"I have, I been there before," Stan answered.

"You lying, Stan, you ain't never been to the Hamp," I said, exiting the highway onto Flat Shoals Road.

East Hampton Apartments was a gated community with a security guard. Not like the gated communities near where we lived, where the gates protected valuable estates. This community was clearly violent and infamous for its drug trade. When I pulled up to the security gate, the security guard looked me over long and hard from his booth. He hit a button and the gate lifted before he nodded me into the complex. He knew why I was there. As a matter of fact, cars were already lined up behind me, almost all those cars were there for the same reasons. I knew the security guard was wondering how a kid my age was driving, let alone how I could be pulling up in a brand-new car.

We drove on into the apartment complex, and no sooner had we crossed over the first speed bump than groups of young black men were already flagging us down. Some even ran up to the car.

"Got them pillows shawty," they advertised.

"Pillows" was slang for fat bags of weed because they were fluffy, like pillows.

The weed dealers were aggressive because the competition was great in the Hamp. Everybody had weed. I parked alongside an apartment building and Big Mark let down his window. He asked one of the dealers at the window for a twenty sack. The young man ran to the bushes near an apartment corridor and pulled out a large Ziploc bag filled to the brim with smaller Ziploc bags inside. He pulled two bags out and handed them to Big Mark in the back. Mark gave him the twenty dollar bill.

I pulled off from there. I had never been in such an intense drug arena. I lived in the projects, but the Hamp made where I lived seem like a kids' park. We jumped on Interstate 85 North headed back home, and I was relieved that we had made it out of the Hamp alive. But that relief was short-lived when I spotted the police in my rearview mirror. I knew this wasn't a good sign. I could see the officer running the car's tag numbers into his computer. The car was stolen, and so were the tags.

"The police behind us," I said as calm as possible.

"Don't look back," Brad said.

Immediately, Big Mark and Stan looked back.

In an instant, the cop cut on his blue swirling lights.

"What should I do?" I asked. I was genuinely lost for ideas.

"Ride out!" Big Mark yelled.

"We can't outrun no police radios," Stan added.

In seconds, there were two more police cruisers behind us. Mark tossed the marijuana out the window. The police cruisers boxed me in and forced me off the road to emergency lanes. No sooner had I thrown the car in park than the police jumped out of their vehicles and surrounded the car with their guns drawn.

"Put your fucking hands in the air, now!" they exclaimed.

I put my hands up, and they snatched me from the car like a bag of trash. They slammed me on the concrete with great force.

"You fucking faggots like to steal cars?" an officer screamed in my ear while he rummaged my pockets.

As I lay on the ground, I could see that Stan, Big Mark, and Brad were getting the same treatment. I was cuffed and thrown head first into the back of a police cruiser.

The next time I saw Mark, Brad, and Stan we were all in the police station's holding tank. They kept us separated and interrogated us all separately. They grilled us for information as to how we got the car. This lasted six hours straight. Nobody was willing to talk; we all practiced the code. Don't snitch. Since I was the driver, they charged me with theft by taking for stealing the car.

I slept on the hard concrete bench of the holding tank until four o'clock in the morning. It was then that an officer woke me up and took me out to my mother, who was waiting in the lobby of the jail. Her face was stern, and her disappointment was obvious. As soon as I was close to her, she grabbed me by the back of the neck and ushered me out of the precinct.

"So, this is all you can think to do while I'm at work!" she screamed as we rode home.

I kept my gaze out the passenger's window. I dreaded to look at her.

"Oh, you don't have anything to say now, huh? I know one thing, you better not leave that house for a month. If I catch you outside with any of those punks you run with, I'm going to beat the paint off you."

She didn't say anything else.

Chapter Four

Eventually, I was set a court date for the crime of joyriding, and we all three ended up getting two years' probation for our auto theft crimes. This was the beginning of my criminal career. Probation meant nothing to me or any of the other guys. We continued living our lives in the same manner with no regard for our brief brush with the law.

No matter how much money Brad, Big Mark, Stan and I made, and no matter how far we could travel, I still found myself paying more attention to what the older guys in the neighborhood were doing. The older dudes would talk to us sometimes when they needed someone to run to the store or to be a lookout while they hustled.

Neighborhood football games were a weekend event in the projects. The older dudes liked to gamble on the games. The girls in the neighborhood used to like to watch the games. It was during these games that I began to pay attention to one girl, her name was Bonnie. Bonnie was about eight years older than me, but that didn't stop me from noticing how attractive she was. She wore cut off jean shorts that were frayed at the ends. I remember the shorts vividly because of how they showed off her velvety thighs and ample buttocks. I can't remember ever seeing her wear anything else.

I quickly developed a crush on Bonnie, and every play I made during the football game I did so that she would notice. I always tried to make eye contact with her, but she never responded. I'm certain it had a lot to do with the fact that she looked at me as a child. After all, every time she saw me, I was with Brad, Stan, and Mark.

L caught me staring at Bonnie one day after a game and pulled me to the side.

"You like Bonnie?" he said.

I looked at her longingly from afar.

"Yeah I like her, she fine," I said.

"Bonnie like dudes who getting money," L said. "You getting money?"

"A lil bit," I replied.

He shook his head and smiled. "A lil bit ain't gonna cut it with Bonnie," he said. "Meet me in front of my building at nine o'clock tonight, and I'll show you how to get a lot of money."

Without the slightest hesitance, I agreed to be there at nine. It was no problem for me to meet with L at nine p.m. because my mother would be at work. She worked two jobs, so most days I would be asleep before she even got home. That night, I found L and four others standing in a group in front of their apartment building. They were always hanging out in front of the building until the early morning hours. Every day was a party with those guys. They never worked but stayed with the latest clothes and sneakers. Any of them could pull a bank roll out of his pocket at a moment's notice.

30

"What up, Ken?" L said as I walked up to the group. He was smoking a joint and swirling a plastic cup half filled with cognac in his hand.

"You ready to get to the money?"

I nodded.

"Rocco, hook the lil homey up," L said to one of the men standing behind him.

Rocco was his right-hand man. They were always together. Rocco was brown skinned with a low Caesar haircut. He had an athletic build and wore Mitchell and Ness basketball jerseys every day. He wore jerseys more than the athletes whose names were stitched on the back of them.

I followed Rocco into an apartment a few feet away from where everyone was gathered.

"Wait right here," he said as he headed toward the back rooms.

I stood in the living room staring at my feet, not really understanding what I was about to get involved in after that. What I did know was that money was involved and that I would soon become better acquainted with L and his associates. More important than all these things was the idea that maybe now Bonnie would notice me.

Rocco came back and dumped a handful of small blue baggies in my hand. I stared at the bags and the little hard, white squares inside them.

"That's ten sacks nigga," Rocco said. "Bring us back eighty dollars. You keep the twenty."

I nodded, but I didn't really know what he meant.

"You ready to go to work?" L asked when I came back outside.

"I'm ready," I told him.

That night, I hung out all night with L. I waited in the breezeway for crack smokers to walk up and buy crack. Business was booming. I sold every bag I had in two hours and went home twenty dollars richer. After that first night, life was different for me. I wasn't with Brad, Mike, and Stan as much as I used to be since meeting L. I was spending a lot more time with L and his friends. I made more money and had more fun. I also got to see Bonnie more often.

It wasn't long after I began selling crack cocaine that I learned about Bonnie's addiction. She showed up to buy crack daily. The thing about Bonnie was that she almost never had to pay for her drugs. Bonnie was eighteen and had the youthful vigor and body to match. She was a cute girl, and a sexual favor in exchange for a ten dollar bag was a fair trade.

One day, Bonnie came to the building looking to get high. At the time I was the only one at the building. I was sitting on the stairs in the breezeway.

"Where everybody at?" she asked, placing her hands on her full hips.

The cut off blue jean shorts she wore were tight around the thighs.

I shrugged. "I don't know where them dudes at, I'm here though. What's up?" I said.

She looked me up and down.

"I'm trying smoke," she said.

My heart began to beat harder. I knew this was my chance to make a move.

"How much money you got?"

She squeezed two fingers into her fitted front pocket and pulled out a five dollar bill.

I shook my head. "That's not enough," I said.

"Well, that's all I got, little boy!" she snapped.

I looked her up and down long and hard, letting her know my intentions with my eyes.

"I can take care of you, though. If you take care of me."

She smirked in disbelief. "Take care of you how?"

"I got the keys to the crib," I said, pointing towards L's apartment door.

"Let's go in and do it real quick. I'll break you off a dub."

She thought about it. I went into my pocket and pulled out a twenty dollar sack of crack. I let it sit in the flat of my hand so that she could see it.

Begrudgingly, she said, "Come on, lil boy, you got 10 minutes."

I came off the stairs swiftly and fished the apartment key from my pocket. I opened the apartment door and we went into the den. She sat on the couch, and I sat down next to her completely lost as to what to do next. I had never had sex before, ever. I took off my shirt and shoes. After that, Bonnie took over everything. She stood up in front of me and wiggled out of her shorts. Her panties were red and lacey. I sat staring at her thighs in a lustful stupor.

"You going to take your pants off or not?" she asked.

I quickly slid my pants and boxers down to my ankles. She took off her panties and straddled me on the couch. She guided my erection into her vagina and, in just a little over forty seconds, I was no longer a virgin.

As the weeks passed, I was on the block more often, and by myself. I had basically become the perfect worker for L and his crew. This freed them up to do other things. They would leave the projects at around ten p.m. and wouldn't return until three or four a.m. Every time they came back, they had pockets full of money. I could never put my finger on what they were doing, so one night I asked.

"We making big boy moves, Ken. You ain't ready for this lifestyle," L said as he sat on the stairs in the breezeway counting a stack of money in his lap.

I took offense to him calling me a kid.

"I was born ready," I said. "What I gotta do?"

L looked up from his counting and stared at me hard. The smile left his face.

"You ever shot a gun?" he asked.

I thought back to the time when I saw my mom's gun lying in her lap when we were leaving Tifton. I knew where she kept it now, it was put up in her closet. I would sometimes take it down and point it at my reflection in the mirror. That was the closest I had ever come to firing it though.

So I answered, "Of course."

"OK, we'll see what you can do," L said before starting to recount his money again.

The next morning, as soon as my mom left for work, I was in her closet. I pulled her .380 handgun from its box on the top shelf of the closet. I hurried to my room. I sat on the bed, loading and unloading the

35

clip of the gun. Then I put the clip into the gun and pulled the slide, loading a bullet into the chamber. I aimed at the wall with my finger placed lightly on the trigger. I knew that if I applied a little bit of pressure I would certainly fire the weapon. I kept practicing pulling the trigger and, without warning, the gun went off right then. A loud bang echoed throughout the apartment. My eyes grew as wide as silver dollar coins, and my heart landed in my stomach. Before I had a chance to regain my composure, my younger sister stuck her head in my doorway. She looked around the room bewildered, then she spotted the gun in my hand.

"I'm telling!" she said without hesitation.

"No, don't tell," I said, grabbing her arm before she could leave. "It was an accident. I'll give you twenty dollars if you don't tell."

She jerked her arm away from me and held her hand out, waiting for the money. I went to my dresser drawer and gave her a twenty dollar bill from my bankroll. She snatched it, and said, "I'm still telling," before bolting out of the room.

I didn't have the energy to play. I searched the room for where the bullet had struck, and right next to my closet door was a small bullet hole. It wasn't so obvious that my mom would see it or know what it was. I quickly took the gun back to my mother's room and placed it back in its box and at the top of the closet just as I had found it. It was official, now I could say I had shot a gun.

36

Chapter Five

I didn't attend church as much as I had when I lived in Tifton with my grandparents, but the church was still a part of my life. Every Sunday my mom went to church, and if I didn't wake up and leave the house before she started getting ready for church, then I would have to put my clothes on and go too.

I didn't like the idea of missing what was happening in my neighborhood while I was at church. But at the same time, it was the only time I got to see my friend Josh from my old neighborhood in Lawrenceville. I would see him and his family at church whenever I did go. His mother always took an interest in how I was doing. She would always ask if I was staying out of trouble, and I would always tell her that I was.

Josh and I used to talk after church and try to catch up on each other's lives. It was apparent that he was living a different life than I was. I talked about weed and stealing cars; he talked about school and his future. At the same time, he was enjoying himself and, although I had a different outlook on life, I was having a good time as well.

I was sitting on the steps in front of L's apartment one evening, serving my usual customers. I hadn't seen L since he promised me that he would take me with him and his crew on one of their late-night runs. I was eager to know what they were doing. I wasn't as concerned with the money they were coming back with as much as I was with what it took to get the money. I didn't like the feeling of being left out of anything.

L came out of his apartment with Rocco close behind him. They were dressed in dark clothing, just like they always were when they left for their night hustle.

"You riding with us tonight?" L asked as soon as he saw me.

"I'm ready," I said.

I got up and followed them to L's car. It was a dark gray 1973 Chevy Caprice Classic convertible with a black rag top. It was clean and still had the factory wheels. I hopped in the back seat. We rode south for about thirty minutes. I had no idea where we were going, but I didn't mind. I was fine with riding. There were other kids my age in the neighborhood, but none of them had established the type of relationship that I had with L and his team.

We ended up in a small city on the outskirts of Atlanta in a predominately white neighborhood. We drove down a stretch of highway that was busy with late night bars and restaurants. L and Rocco spoke with each other in low, hushed tones while pointing at specific points on the highway. I sat back in my seat trying to make sense of what was about to happen.

"You good back there?" L asked.

"I'm good," I replied.

L pulled into a parking lot and parked in the lot full of vehicles with the engine running. We had pulled onto the property of a bar. All the patrons going in and or leaving were white.

"Alright little homey," L said, adjusting his rear view so that he could see me. "We here. This is what we do. A lot of these white folks leave the bar drunk and walk home. We catch one of them slipping, and we lay um down."

Rocco handed me a black pistol from over the front seat. I grabbed the pistol and held it in my lap. It was bigger than my mom's gun. I had never robbed anyone before, but at least I had experience with guns. I had asked to be here, and now I had to live up to my word.

"You want me to kill um too?" I asked.

L turned all the way around in his seat with his face frowned up bad.

"Hell, nah Ken! We just taking money, not lives," he shot back.

He tossed a black bandanna onto the back seat. "Tie that around your mouth," he said.

I grabbed the rag off the seat and tied it around my mouth. I felt ready. I felt respected. L pulled out of the parking space, drove around the block and parked on a dark side street not far from the bar property.

"Anybody walk up through here, we going to lay um down," Rocco said. "You ready? You ain't scared, are you?"

I pulled the rag down from my mouth.

"I'm ready," I said triumphantly while fondling the safety on the pistol.

Rocco tied his rag around his mouth and got out the car. I got out and followed Rocco down the street back towards the bar. We ran crouched low to the ground with the bottom half of our faces covered with bandanas. I felt like I was in a movie, I was nervous and entertained at the same time.

L stayed in the car. Rocco and I found a dark corner alongside a house about a block away from our getaway vehicle. I followed Rocco's every move. It was clear this wasn't his first job. He was quiet as we crouched low in the darkness, his eyes darting up and down the street in search of a victim.

After about twenty minutes of wait time, we heard a man and woman laughing and chatting in the distance. They were oblivious to the danger lurking in the dark recesses of their neighborhood. In a short moment, we spotted the couple strolling casually down the sidewalk hand in hand. Rocco didn't talk; as soon as the couple was in eyesight, he ran up on them with his gun drawn. I followed him closely.

I watched as the eyes of the victims grew wide with fear as two armed black men appeared, as if from nowhere, with guns drawn. The woman gasped loudly, her scream suffocated by fear. Their hands went up quickly and the woman's purse dropped to the concrete. Immediately, Rocco was in the man's pockets. I picked up the purse. Rocco had them take off their jewelry. They handed their jewels to him. It took less than a minute to take everything they had on them. We ran back down the block towards the car. The couple remained stark still, watching our backs as we ran away before disappearing into the night. They were in shock. There were no words spoken, everything just happened. Guns speak for themselves.

We hopped in the car and L skidded off into the night. He quickly turned corners and raced down streets until we were about ten minutes from the crime scene. When we were on the expressway, L let out a holler and began banging on the steering wheel. He was pumped, the thrill of the robbery had him on high. He and Rocco slapped hands in the front seat.

"You good, Ken?" L asked.

"I'm good," I said with the woman's purse still in my lap.

Rocco looked back over the front seat.

"Why the fuck you still got the purse?" he yelled.

I shrugged, at a loss for words. L pulled the car over, coming to a screeching halt.

"Gimme me the purse," Rocco said.

I handed him the purse and he quickly rummaged through it. In a

41

few short seconds, he had tossed the purse out the window and we were back on the road.

Back at L's apartment, L got out the car and removed the stolen license plate before replacing it with the legitimate one. We went inside his apartment and we all sat on the couch. Rocco dumped a gold watch, two diamond rings and three hundred dollars cash onto the coffee table, this being all the loot acquired from the heist.

L stood up and lit a joint.

"So now you see how we get down," he said to me. "You didn't do bad for a first timer."

He counted out a hundred dollars from the money on the table and handed it to me.

"Appreciate it," I said.

"What you going to do with all that money?" Rocco asked.

I shrugged.

"What you doing this weekend, Ken?" L asked.

"Nothing, what's up?" I replied.

"We need somebody to drive this weekend. We going to Freaknik. Let you spend some of that money."

"What's Freaknik?" I asked.

"A giant freak party," Rocco said as he hit the joint.

"More bitches than you can imagine, it's the ultimate party," L added, staring off into the distance as if he was already there.

"College girls from all over the country coming to the 'A' to party for spring break."

I stood up and stuffed my money into my jeans pocket. L walked me over to the door with his hand on my shoulder. "Good job, today, Lil G," he said. "See you tomorrow."

I turned to walk away, then stopped in my tracks. "Why you call me Lil G?" I asked.

"Oh, that stands for Lil Gangster," he said.

I walked home in the morning darkness contemplating the robbery. It was fun, it was easy, it paid, and I was a part of the team. All I could think about now was Freaknik.

Friday rolled around and I met up with L and Rocco at ten in the morning. It was the day that Freaknik was supposed to begin. When I got to L's building, the first thing I noticed was the Chevy Caprice Classic. It was totally transformed. It had a wet blue metallic paint job. The accents were shiny chrome to match the massive twenty-inch wheels. I banged on L's door, my eyes never leaving the car. L opened the door, dressed up like he was in a rap video. His sneakers were new, and his jewelry was shining. I even noticed that he wore one of the rings from the robbery just two nights before. Rocco was dressed in new gear as well, new sneakers and a throwback Hawks jersey. L tossed me the keys. We hopped in the Caprice and rode towards downtown Atlanta.

It was clear that the city was buzzing. Almost every other license plate we passed was from another state, Virginia, North Carolina, Tennessee, Florida, New York. Every car was loaded with girls, and it wasn't even noon yet. We drove to Lenox Mall; I had to get my swag up to match the fly of L and Rocco. I bought jean shorts, a polo shirt, and the new Nike Air Huaraches. Then we continued downtown. Once we hit downtown, we stopped at the IHOP for brunch.

The parking lot of the IHOP was already full when we got there, and the cars were just as fabulous as ours. It was like a car show in the parking lot. The restaurant was filled with people; it was as active as a nightclub inside. Girls were dressed scantily and willing to engage in conversation. Everyone was making plans for meeting up later in the evening. We ate and conversed with a lot of women while in the IHOP, and before we knew it, it was already 2 p.m.

We left IHOP and hopped back in the Caprice. I pulled off the property and the crowd in the city streets had grown tenfold. It was bumper to bumper traffic. The streets were swarming with college students. I turned up the sounds in our car while Rocco and L hung out the window hollering at girls. The difference between this day and the other days we tried to talk to girls was that the girls were all receptive. They were from other states, and they were all visiting the city looking

44

for a good time. They would walk up to the Caprice, lean in, look at me and say, "Y'all got that little boy driving!" Some got in and rode for a block or so. We had as many as six girls in the car at times.

We had plenty of Hennessy and weed to ride with for the day. It was taking almost thirty minutes to an hour just to drive from one block to the next block due to the party traffic. By 6 p.m., the party was literally in the middle of the streets. When we finally made it to Five Points Underground Atlanta, the traffic was at a standstill. People had resorted to leaving their cars and partying in the streets. Everyone's radio was at max volume. Women were standing on top of cars in the shortest of shorts, dancing and gyrating to the music. If a car had a sunroof, it had women hanging out of it. If the car was a drop top, women were sitting up on the back seats, and vans cruised with the side doors slid wide open.

Sometimes the women would strip completely naked and dance in the open. When this happened, men would surround them with video cameras to record the experience. I had never seen anything like what I witnessed on that night. The police weren't able to do anything but spectate. They hadn't prepared for a party of this magnitude, a blissful anarchy soon consumed the city. It was only Friday, and Freaknik had officially taken over the city.

When I moved to Atlanta from Tifton, I hadn't known what to expect, but as I sat in the driver's seat, watching the ultimate party transpire, I almost couldn't believe I was amongst it all. I was driving

45

what would be every teenager's dream car. The rims and paint job on the Chevy made chicks flock to us. I was doing exactly what I wanted. Life couldn't have been any better at that moment. I wondered what Josh was doing. I couldn't wait to tell him about Freaknik.

The party continued in this exact fashion all the way into Saturday evening. As a grand finale, L and Rocco decided to take me to the infamous Stewart Avenue. Stewart Avenue was a popular prostitution strip. L wanted to repay me for driving the entire weekend. We pulled up to a seedy hotel at around 3 a.m. It was called the Alamo. It was designed to look like the historic Alamo in San Antonio, Texas. We pulled up and parked. Several ladies walked up to the car in miniskirts and revealing low-cut tops. L and Rocco quickly chose the ladies they would be spending the next hour with right then. They told me to pick one. I did.

I ended up in a closet-sized room with a big-breasted chocolate woman. She was a grown woman in every sense of the word, and my erection grew just from the sight of the way her plump ass peeked from under her red miniskirt. In the room I was silent. I hadn't ever been in this situation. I sat on the bed while she pulled her top over her head.

"How old are you?" she asked incredulously while she got on her knees and worked my belt loose.

"I'm twenty-one." I lied expertly.

I had been telling this exact story all weekend.

46

No sooner had I had lied than she was pulling my pants down quick. She looked up at me, I looked down at her, and then we both looked at my boxers. My boxers were decorated with Transformers.

Chapter Six

After Freaknik weekend, everybody in the neighborhood was looking forward to the summer. A skating rink named Sparkles was the happening thing to do on Sunday nights. Before I had a chance to go to the rink myself, I was already hearing stories about the place. Many of the stories I heard about Sparkles ended with a brawl at the end of any given night. Rival neighborhoods often clashed at the skating rink, most times before the skating rink's actual closing time. I told L that I was riding with him to Sparkles the next Sunday, and it was all that I could think about up until that day.

We got to Sparkles about six in the evening. As soon as we got out the Caprice, you could feel the tension in the air as we crossed the parking lot to the rink. We caught glares from the other guys lined up in the lot posted up in front of their cars. Some had their trunks open so that their boxed speakers could thump out loud. L and I slapped fives with those we recognized. The girls were out, too, in their cut off jean shorts. They cackled loudly, most of them just enjoying the vibes from the music blaring from the cars. All of them savoring attention.

Inside, the DJ was spinning the latest hits by TLC, SWV, 2pac, Playa Poncho, and even Edward J. Sitting at a table in the crowded dining area were two Spanish guys and a white girl. They looked to be in their mid-teens. L walked right up to the shorter of the two and the two of them slapped hands. L introduced me to the two Mexicans, the shorter of the two was named Levi. The other persons at the table were his brother Jay and Jay's girlfriend Lisa.

I watched as L and Levi carried on like long-lost comrades. After a few moments, they walked towards the bathrooms. I followed behind them. In the bathroom, Levi went into his waistband and pulled out a small sandwich bag filled halfway with cocaine. He stepped into a stall and dipped out a good amount with just his cuffed fingers, he made several lines on top of the toilet paper holder encasement, and one by one we all went into the stall and did a line. This was the first time I had snorted cocaine. I hadn't even known that you could use the drug in its soft form. All I had seen up to this point was the hard version.

I didn't really feel much different after snorting my first line. Then again, I didn't know much of anything at twelve years old. When I first moved to the projects, my life had begun to change, but the beginning of the end started when I met Levi and his brother Jay.

When we left the bathroom, we all headed back to the dining area. It seemed as if only the girls were skating, while most of the males in the rink were there just to talk to the girls. Levi was talking louder than the rest of us and arguing with almost anyone who passed our table. L was laughing at him and his antics the entire night, clearly amused by his temper. After several confrontations, Levi finally got what he was looking for that night. He had started an argument with a slender black guy with an afro from across the room. Levi threw up his hands and stood up abruptly, his chair flipping over onto its back. He argued from a distance at first, Levi claiming that he was being stared at by the guy. Eventually, the guy with the afro approached our table, followed by his crew of about three people. As soon as he approached our table, Levi was throwing punches.

L threw a punch at another person. Once I saw L jump in, it was go time. So I jumped in too. Then others joined, and the next thing we knew the entire dining area was in an uproar. The music stopped and the DJ pleaded for calm over the mic. The tables in the dining area were soon flipped over, and everyone scattered toward the nearest exits. Quickly, the fight carried over out into parking lot outside. I was swinging at anyone I didn't recognize, and a short moment later we heard police sirens. Everybody hustled to their cars. In the melee, I lost sight of L, but I spotted Levi running. Instinctively, I followed him. He ran to a fire red, low rider truck sitting on twenty-inch chrome wheels. He jumped inside and cranked the engine, and I dived in the bed of the truck. I saw him look back at me through his rearview. He recognized me and pulled off as I lay down in the bed of the truck.

The truck pulled off aggressively and made several erratic brakes and turns. As I rolled around in the bed of the truck, I heard gunshots ring out fast. The bangs were deafening and close, I knew they were coming from inside the truck. I was lying down in the rear, bouncing around like a tennis ball. But oddly enough, I wasn't scared at all. In fact, I was having the time of my life. The only thing I regretted was not having a gun to shoot for myself.

After about five minutes, the truck came to a grinding halt. I sat up and looked to see where we were.

"Get the fuck in the car!" Levi screamed out the driver's window.

I quickly hopped out the back and got in the front. Levi peeled out.

"Where the hell is my brother?" he asked, more to himself than to me.

I spotted a black nine-millimeter hand gun down on the floor board.

"Stupid!" he said, slapping the steering wheel with the palm of his hand.

"You live close by L?" he asked.

"Yep, the same complex," I said.

Levi calmed down in record time, he cut up the music letting his 15-inch speakers beat. We hopped on the interstate and headed towards my neighborhood as if we hadn't just been in a gang fight or what could have very well have been a deadly shoot-out that night.

When we finally got to my apartment complex, L and a few other guys from the neighborhood were hanging out in the breezeway in front of L's apartment. I could tell by L's hand movements and body language that he was telling the story about what had just happened at the skating rink. When Levi and I got out of the truck, we all slapped hands and laughed at what had just transpired. "Did I get any of them bitches?" Levi asked. "I didn't care who I hit," he said laughing.

Levi showed no remorse for shooting into a crowd of people, and I admired that. So did L.

"I told y'all he was loco," L said.

Everyone erupted in laughter.

"Y'all wanna come by my house now? We can drink and get high there," Levi suggested.

L readily agreed. We hopped in the Caprice and followed Levi to his house.

L told me more about Levi during our drive to Levi's house. Levi's father had been a notorious drug kingpin who was violently murdered when Levi was fourteen and his brother only twelve. Levi hadn't been mentally right ever since. If the rage I had seen him display only an hour before was any indication as to how he acted on a regular basis, then I had no choice except to believe everything L was telling me.

When we pulled up to the winding driveway of the mini mansion sitting up on a hill, there was no denying that L was telling the truth about Levi. I had never seen a house this big before in my life.

"This dude rich for real," I said in awe.

I wondered why a person who lived in a house like this one would be running the streets with no fear of losing his freedom and trigger happy on top of that. It looked as if he already had everything we were hustling for daily.

"I told you his dad had that dope money," L replied as we followed Levi up the driveway before parking in front of the three-car garage. L threw the car in park.

"His dad was murdered by his uncle about some money. That's why he crazy," he explained.

We got out and met with Levi in the driveway. As we walked to the front door of the house, we saw headlights ascending from the street below. Levi quickly pulled his gun from his waistband and held it gripped down by his side. I recognized that his first reaction to everything was to pull out his pistol. The closer the lights came the more intense the moment grew. I scanned the large yard looking for a path, just in case I had to run. After a moment, Levi's grip on his pistol relaxed. "Oh, that's just my mom," he said.

The powder-blue Benz pulled up and parked in front of one of the garage doors. Levi's mother, sister, and brother got out the car, followed by Jay's girlfriend Lisa. We hadn't seen Jay or Lisa since we had fled the skating rink. When the mom and sister exited the car, L nudged me lightly on my arm, and I knew exactly what he was getting at. Levi's mother and sister were very attractive Latino women. Voluptuous with pouty lips and perfectly shaped hips. The daughter was the spitting image of her mother. I had love in my eyes.

Jay was highly upset.

"Why the fuck did you leave me?" he yelled at Levi, getting in his face.

Levi jumped at him as if he was about to hit him, and Jay cowered away. It was clear that Jay was intimidated by his older brother and for good reason.

His mom yelled at them both in Spanish, and they continued arguing in Spanish all the way into the house. The interior of the house didn't disappoint. There were leather couches and big screen TVs throughout the home. Crystal chandeliers, expensive paintings, and vases decorated the house. There were a pool and a basketball court in the rear. You could see the drug game had been lucrative for both Levi and his family.

L, Levi, and I ended up in the sunken den. Levi pulled a bag of powdered cocaine from a drawer in the coffee table. He poured a hefty amount onto a silver dinner plate that sat in the center of the coffee table. He made three lines, and we all snorted.

"I like your style, Levi," L said. "You ain't scared to use that strap."

Levi nodded. "My father taught me how to shoot a gun when I was six," he said. "He told me that if something ever happened to him it was my job to keep the family together. That's what I'm going to do," he said as a matter of fact and before separating three more lines. We snorted.

Levi leaned back in the couch and pinched his nose and squeezed his eyes tight. He sat up quickly and shook his head left to right.

He really is crazy, I thought to myself.

"I've been having problems with these niggas on the south side," Levi said suddenly, after his moment. "I need some help when I go see about these dudes. We can lay them down and split the loot. They got that bread for real."

"Oh, without question, you know I'm with it," L said before slapping hands with Levi. "I know Lil G ready too."

"You already know I'm ready," I replied.

Feeling the effects of the cocaine at this point, I truly was ready to do whatever they had planned. The cocaine made me realize how much of a gangster I really was. I had just turned thirteen and was already having meetings with Latin gangsters in mansions. I thought about Josh. I wondered what he was doing, probably sleeping this time of night.

"Yo, why they call you Lil G?" Levi asked, snatching me from my thoughts.

Before I could reply, L answered for me. "Oh, that stands for Little Gangster."

Levi looked at me and I saw his mind racing. I knew he was thinking about how I had handled myself at the skating rink.

"Lil G," he said in approval.

Chapter Seven

I ended up staying at Levi's house for nine days straight. We snorted coke, smoked weed, drank liquor, and played video games most of those hours. It was on the ninth day that I decided to go home to get the rest of my belongings. Levi and his family made it clear that I could stay for as long as I liked. They had plenty of room in their home. His mother never questioned or bothered Levi about anything he did. He had been adamant about us moving in with him the entire nine days we were there. All we did was have fun, not to mention that I was growing increasingly fond of his younger sister, Jennifer. I hadn't expected to hit it off with her so well. But it felt like we had been friends much longer than the few days we had known each other.

It was a Tuesday morning when I decided to stop by my mother's house so that I could get my clothing. I wanted to get in and out of the apartment early while my mom was at work and my siblings were at school. Jennifer wanted to ride with me to get my things. We were inseparable already, she even got her aunt to drive me home. I think she feared me leaving and not coming back.

When we arrived at my apartment complex, I had her aunt park two buildings away from the one I lived in with my family. Meanwhile, I scanned the parking lot up and down for my mother's car. Feeling confident that I could get in and out of the apartment undetected, I walked up to my door and pulled my house key from my pocket. I quietly slipped in the front door. Although I knew that my mom wasn't home, I still entered cautiously. I hadn't been home or seen my mother in about ten days. I dreaded what that encounter would be like when I did see her. The apartment was quiet and still; I grew confident as I made my way past the living room to my bedroom. I had just crossed the threshold of my doorway when my oldest sister Pam appeared at the end of the hallway.

I jumped, startled that she was home. She stood staring at me bewildered.

"Kenyatta!" she yelled. "Are you crazy?"

I stood motionless. I wasn't prepared to see anyone or answer any questions.

"Where have you been?" she asked in distress, her eyes beginning to water. "Mommy has been worried about you. She was crying and everything!"

I proceeded on into my room and to my closet. I pulled my school backpack from the closet. I removed the books that were inside and walked over to my dresser to begin filling the bag with clothes. I still couldn't find words to speak now.

My sister came in the room, put her hand on my shoulder, and spun me around roughly so that I had to look directly into her face. Her tears were now rolling down her face.

"Did you hear me?" she asked. "I said Mom has been worried about you. She was even crying." She wiped her eyes.

"You're only thirteen, Kenyatta, you're still a little boy. I know you hang out with the old fools, but I don't see their mommas crying. I only see ours. What about Grandma, what about Granddad? You have an entire family worried about you! "

I turned back to the dresser and started stuffing clothes into my bag. I knew my mom had been looking for me. I even knew how old I was, but I was having a good time with my friends, and honestly I didn't see the harm in that.

"Tell Mama that I'll see her soon," I said nonchalantly.

I was truly more concerned about what was going on back at Levi's house. I did miss my mom, but I reasoned that she was worried for nothing, I was OK. At least my sister could tell her that she had seen me. Maybe she wouldn't cry after that.

"Do you love Mama?"

"Of course, I do," I insisted.

"Then come home," she pleaded.

My little sister Kenya came into the bedroom, a blanket was draped over her shoulders. She looked under the weather. I assumed the reason they were home was that Pam had stayed home to take care of her.

"Mommy been looking for you," Kenya said to me.

The sincerity in her voice made me want to stay home. My entire being told me to stay home. I thought about Jennifer sitting in the car waiting for me. I thought about the fun I had had with her and my friends at the mansion. I looked at the both of my sisters and said, "OK, I'll stay."

They were genuinely happy. They both embraced me. After a few moments, I broke away from them.

"What time will Mama be home?" I asked.

"When I call and tell her you're home," Pam said excitedly, already headed for the house phone.

I smiled. "OK, I'm going to take a quick shower," I said, ushering them both out the room.

I began unbuttoning my shirt as if I was undressing while I closed the door. I waited a few seconds then grabbed my book bag full of clothes and hopped out the bedroom window. I ran back towards where Jennifer and her aunt were waiting. I jumped in, and we headed back to the mansion.

When we got back to Jennifer and Levi's home, I found Levi, L, and Rocco in the game room shooting pool.

"Lil G, welcome back!" Levi said, tossing me a fresh Heineken from the mini fridge.

L and Rocco were sitting on a black leather sofa; L was separating lines of coke from a small pile of coke on the glass coffee table in front of them. Rocco got up and let me sit down so that I could do a line. I snorted a healthy line. The things my sister had told me about my mother and her concern for me replayed over and over in my head. I felt guilty that I had lied and said that I was going to stay. I imagined how sad they would all be when they saw that I had left. I felt the cocaine drain down the back of my throat, and nothing seemed to worry me anymore. As a matter of fact, life was good.

"So, where they at now?" I heard Rocco ask Levi.

"On Buford Highway," Levi replied before lining up his pool cue for a corner pocket shot.

"So, we just going to catch them outside and drive by?" L asked.

Levi added chalk to his cue. "L, you drive," he said. "Rocco, me, and Lil G, we'll let them shots fly."

Rocco nodded in agreement. "I'm with it," he said.

L and I agreed as well. We all did a couple more lines before we loaded up in the Caprice. Rocco and I rode in the back, L was the driver, and Levi rode shotgun.

Levi gave L directions from the passenger's seat. All three of us had a handgun, and we were all ready to use them. During the drive, Levi told us an entire story about an issue he had with some cholos from

61

Buford Highway. He ranted about being disrespected. He spoke about his father's murder. He was angry but for no one reason. Still, by the time we reached Buford Highway, I was just as furious as Levi. We had all formed a strong bond over the last two weeks. We were one another's family, and I was eager to prove my loyalty.

Levi navigated us to an apartment complex about a mile off the highway. It was a lower-income neighborhood, and the Latino presence was dominant. It was 3:00 in the afternoon, so there were people milling about. Kids were getting out of school, teenagers were grouped in bunches chatting, and others sat out on cars. We crept through the neighborhood while Levi peered into the daily activities of these unsuspecting bystanders from the passenger's seat, looking for a specific person. We were well into the belly of the apartment complex when Levi's brow narrowed. "There they go right there," he said, sinking down into his seat.

"Go down to the end of the complex and turn around," he instructed L.

L drove by the group of Latino men casually. I watched from the backseat, eyeing the group of men with disdain as if they had done something to me personally. L made a U-turn. The apartment complex was one way in and one way out of there. After the U-turn, we were facing out of the complex. The group of cholos was up ahead, only one hundred feet from where we sat. We inspected our guns, making sure they were loaded. On Levi's command, L punched the gas and sped towards the men. We let our windows down and started firing at the crowd. The men quickly took cover. They moved swiftly as if they had suspected we were there for drama since we first rode by. This was their turf, so they disappeared quickly behind cars and buildings as we sped by before falling back into the car after they were aired out.

We made it out of the complex in no time, the tires of the Caprice skidding out as we raced off the property. L made a few quick turns and drove a couple blocks before racing into another apartment complex where he backed the car between two other parked cars. We needed to get off the street for the moment, to let the heat die down. We sat in the car slapping hands and breathing hard. Everything had happened so fast.

"I don't think we hit none of them fools," Levi said, breaking the awkward silence.

Then we all erupted in laughter. We could hear the police sirens in the distance, yet we felt safe. We rolled some weed and did a few lines to relax and kill some time. There was no fear of consequence in the vehicle. In fact, I was so lively that I had an idea.

"I'm ready to do something else," I said.

Levi turned around and look at me over the seat. "What you trying to do, Lil G?" he asked.

"We ain't even shoot nobody," I said. "We already strapped up. Let's hit a lick."

63

Levi turned back around in his seat. "I like Lil G," he said to L.

"Let's go get this money then," L said, starting up the Caprice.

We rode cautiously through the city. We knew the police were out and possibly even looking for our car. We felt invincible though. We made it out past the immediate area of the shooting without incident. We headed north back towards our city. We ended up lurking in a small town where the population of white people was high. We felt like we had a better shot of walking away with some cash if the victim was white.

We were in a quiet residential area. The evening was just beginning to set in the neighborhood when L pulled the Caprice close to the curb discreetly at the top of the neighborhood. I looked around the neighborhood eagerly. The cocaine made me thirsty for an adrenaline high. My gun was resting in my lap, and the weight of it made me feel much older than the thirteen-year-old boy who was sitting there.

Then it happened. A white Cadillac passed us. The Cadillac was brand new. That, along with the neighborhood, we knew that we may have found our mark. It became official when the Cadillac turned into a driveway only three houses away from where we sat. I didn't say anything. I was already out the door as the Cadillac rolled to a stop. I tucked the gun under my shirt and skip-walked hurriedly towards where the Cadillac was parking. The doors of the vehicle opened. I was only twenty yards away. I cut through the grass so that I could get to them before they hit the front door. I met the two white men just as they approached their porch steps. I pulled the gun from up under my shirt and pointed it at the driver. He laid down immediately. And without thought I was already in his pockets. A short second later I heard a slight scuffling above my head. I looked up and saw that Levi had his gun drawn on the passenger, and, at the same time, he was taking a gun from the passenger's hand. In that one moment, I realized that I had just escaped death. If it hadn't been for Levi's presence of mind to follow me, I would have been shot dead by the passenger of the Cadillac.

Chapter Eight

I woke up the next morning to a soothing summer breeze passing over my face. I inhaled deeply as the realization of where I was and how much fun I was having coursed through my mind. I couldn't wait to see what the day had in store. Jennifer was lying next to me still asleep. I got up, threw on gym shorts, and left her room and went out into the hall looking for Levi, L, or Rocco. As I crossed the plush cream carpeting, I knew I had made the right decision by moving out of my mom's house.

I peeked into rooms as I passed by them. The room at the end of the hall was where I saw L's shoes at the door. I walked in to wake him up. When I went in, there was a white girl in bed with him. She sat up quick, she looked nervous, and her face was flushed red from embarrassment. She quickly covered her naked chest with the sheets. I recognized her, it was Lisa, Levi's younger brother's girlfriend. I wondered where Jay was. Somewhere else in the house maybe?

"What's up, Lil G?" L said without so much as a glance in her direction.

I shrugged. "Just seeing what's good. Where the weed at?" I asked.

He pointed to the nightstand. I walked over and grabbed the weed and a loose cigar off the nightstand. I sat on the chaise longue along the wall and grabbed the remote control and cut on the big screen television. No sooner had I begun to break down the cigar than I saw a picture of Levi flash across the screen. The news was showing the exact neighborhood where we had been the day before on Buford Highway. The news reporter had been at the scene of the crime.

He spoke with witnesses in the neighborhood. They could all describe the Caprice perfectly. I looked over at L, whose eyes were as wide as the rims on the Caprice. His mouth hung agape. The television then showed pictures of Rocco and then L. The broadcast continued, connecting the drive-by shooting on Buford Highway with the robbery of two men in the Cadillac. Same car, same description of Levi.

I watched the broadcast as if I was watching a movie. Seeing it made everything that we had done just one day before seem so much more violent and awful than it had been while committing the actual offenses. Ironically, the broadcast never showed a picture of me. I swallowed hard as the segment concluded.

Jennifer appeared in the doorway in tears. She rushed to my side and cried into the nook of my shoulder.

"It's the cocaine!" she whimpered. "It makes you a different person, Kenyatta," she said.

It was obvious she had seen the news.

L snatched the covers off himself.

"Where the fuck is Levi?" he screamed out loud as he pulled on his jeans.

He was moving fast and tripped and fell to the floor while pulling up his pants. When he got them on, he grabbed his shoes and ran down the hallway shouting Levi's name. I pushed Jennifer away from me and followed him. He was opening doors and yelling Levi's name throughout the house, heading downstairs. Rocco came out from a downstairs room rubbing his eyes. He had been woken up by L's incessant yelling.

"What's up?" He asked L.

"Man, we hot!" L said. "They got pictures of me, you, and Levi all over the TV! They got the car description and everything!" he explained, finally getting his shoes on his feet.

"Where the fuck is Levi !" he yelled.

"He and Jay are out together," Jennifer said.

"We need to page them, get them on the phone," L said. "They need to get off the street ASAP! We have to get out of Georgia!"

My mind was racing. Leave the state? Had it come to that?

In thirty minutes, we heard tires screeching in the driveway. In a few short seconds, Levi burst through the front door. Everyone in the house huddled up around the island style kitchen counter. Levi pulled a ziplock bag with cocaine from his pocket and dumped its entire contents onto the marble counter. He nervously separated a line from the pile and snorted it aggressively. He took a moment before he addressed the group.

"I have a connect in Texas, he said. "All we have to do is make it to Texas. We can hustle out there until we make enough money to move on. But we gotta leave the state."

I looked around the room. Everyone was hanging on Levi's every word. The game had changed a little bit. No one in the room could have anticipated this turn of events. L separated out a line, then Rocco and I followed suit. Jay's girlfriend, Lisa, was standing close by L. I wondered if Jay was even bothered by the fact that she was now with L or if he even knew.

"I'm down to ride," Rocco said.

"Me too," I added.

L did another line. "I guess we are moving to Texas," he said.

Levi told us the rest of his plan. They had another property, an even bigger mansion than the one we stood in right then. It was across town about an hour from where we stood. We would hide out there and hustle up enough money to make the move to Texas.

Later that evening, under the cover of darkness, Rocco and L loaded up into the Caprice, and I rode in the truck with Levi. Jennifer and Jay stayed. Lisa hopped in the backseat of the Caprice, she was going with L.

Levi and I spent the hour-long drive talking about our next moves. He explained how happy he was that we would be moving to Texas. He had a cocaine connect out there. He said that we would sell cocaine and live off the profits. I had no reason not to believe him.

When we pulled up to the spiked black gates to our hideout property, I had more reason to believe that I was in good hands. Levi punched a code into a metal box and the gates parted. We followed the driveway up a winding hill. At the top of the hill, the motion detected floodlights lit up the property.

I had never been to the White House, but I imagined it would have looked like the house that was in front of me. It was twice the size of the one we had just left, with marble pillars and a spacious courtyard.

Levi jumped out the truck and we followed him up the cobblestone walk to the porch of the home. He stood on the porch, faced us, and raised his arms.

"Welcome to the hideout!" he said before turning and opening the door.

We all followed him into the foyer. The entryway was massive, high ceilings and chandeliers hung throughout the spacious interior. The mansion was decorated with white leather furniture. Even the bar stools in the kitchen were covered with white leather. The sunken den had a fireplace and a TV as big as the wall. All the appliances throughout were shiny stainless steel. We followed Levi through the home and out onto the rear deck. There was a Jacuzzi on the deck. Beyond the deck below was an Olympic style swimming pool. We continued outside in awe. We took the stairs down from the deck. It was ten p.m., but the lights had the entire golf course size property lit up like it was daytime. We followed Levi to a shed that sat in the distance. He used a key from his ring to unlock the shed. He hit the light switch inside the shed, and we saw that it was filled with dirt bikes, four wheelers, and motorcycles. Rocco slapped hands with L.

"This is what I'm talking about," L said.

Seeing the magnificence of the mansion took our minds off the immediate danger that we faced. Although we knew we were wanted, we also knew that we were in a safe location and we would have more fun here than we had since we met Levi. We went back inside to claim our individual rooms and party.

Jennifer came by the next day with her brother Jay. I was ecstatic about seeing her. It was safe to say I was in love. It was obvious there was tension between Jay and L, this was due to Lisa now being with L. Their slight beef didn't stop us from having the best time of our lives over the next two days. We got high and rode four wheelers and dirt bikes throughout the vast woodlands that made up the property. Music blared from the outdoor speakers, and the alcohol was unlimited. We jumped from the rails of the deck cannonballing into the pool below. Being wanted by the police had never been so much fun.

Although L and Jay did their best to avoid each other, they almost came to blows on our second day at the mansion. Jay was physically not a match for L, and he was Levi's brother. So to keep down disturbances

71

in a time when there were many, L decided to take Lisa home.

Because the Caprice was all over the news, L used Levi's truck to take her home. While he was gone, Rocco, Levi, and I sat out on the deck discussing our move to Texas. We had planned to leave out in two days, on a Friday. We would meet with Levi's cocaine connect, the same connect that had made his father a legend in the dope game. We would get cocaine for the low and sell it for great profit. Levi said that it was in his blood to be a drug lord. From the success his father had seen, I believed him. I ignored the fact that his father had been murdered in cold blood by his own brother.

By the time evening set in, we began to ponder L's absence. He had been gone much longer than it would normally take. We had been paging him on his beeper, but we never got a return call. By the time eight p.m. rolled around, we began to worry. The cocaine made us think the worst, that maybe some of our enemies had caught up with L while he was alone. Levi's truck would make L a target by itself.

By nine, we had loaded up in the Caprice. We left Jennifer and Jay at the mansion in case L came back before we did. We loaded up our guns and rode out. Levi was driving, and it was decided that we would start at the destination L had set out for earlier. We rode the streets with our eyes peeled, looking for Levi's truck, but we didn't see any signs of the truck the entire drive over to Lisa's house.

When we got to Lisa's house, we drove by the single family home cautiously. We didn't see the truck parked out front. The lights in the home were on, but there was no sign of L.

"This is weird as shit," Rocco said.

At the end of the street, we turned around to leave the neighborhood. No sooner had we completed the turn than the entire street behind us lit up with swirling blue lights. My heart sunk to my stomach. I turned around looking out the back window, and I could see nothing but a pinwheel of blue lights.

"Fuck!" Levi yelled.

He punched the gas and the Caprice jolted into action. When I turned around, I saw blue lights approaching us from the front as well. Levi swerved left, dodging the oncoming police cruiser, sidelining a line of parked cars as he completed the maneuver. For the first time in a long time, I was scared. I thought about my mother. Levi was turning up and down streets at an erratic pace; he hopped a curve and drove off the road, barreling over mailboxes as we darted through the streets with no regard for the law.

"Throw the guns out!" he screamed.

I looked around the backseat, there wasn't a gun in sight. The constant bouncing, start and stop of the vehicle during the police chase had caused the guns to become lodged in between and up under the seats.

I heard the helicopter before I saw it. It was directly above us, and I

73

could hear the wind of the propellers. The floodlight raining down from the helicopter was blinding and frightening. My gut told me that we wouldn't be getting out of this situation as easily as we might have hoped. Up until this point, consequences had been far and few between.

The Caprice came to a grinding halt. Levi had turned down a street that dead ended in a cul-de-sac. In seconds, the cops were out of their vehicles and at the doors of the Caprice, guns drawn. We put our hands up on the ceiling of the car and, before my hands were flat, I was already being dragged from the back by my shirt collar. I was slammed on the pavement face first, and, in an instant, I felt the bite of handcuffs on my wrists. I could see Levi and Rocco receiving the same treatment. Rocco was only a few feet over from me. An officer had his knee on his back with his hand holding Rocco's face firmly to the ground.

Rocco made eye contact with me. "Take the gun charges," he mumbled as best he could.

The cop snatched me up and threw me head first into the back of a police cruiser.

I sat up in the back of the police cruiser, sweating profusely. I was nervous, scared, and I didn't know what to expect. I could see that Levi and Rocco were being put into the back of separate vehicles. I reasoned that we would all get out of jail later that day, which was the way it had always been. I wondered what had happened to L.

Almost an hour later, a tall, white cop with a low buzz cut opened the door of the car in which I sat.

"Get out!" he said, aggressively.

I slid out the back of the cruiser, the handcuffs tightening with every move. He spun me around, forcing my back up against the doors. His face was only inches from my own. I could smell his spearmint chewing gum as he spoke.

"I have orders to let you go," he said, menacingly.

He pulled his handcuff key from a ring of many. He spun me around hard, forcing my torso up against the car. He removed the handcuffs before spinning me back around to face him.

"You got 10 seconds to get out of this neighborhood," he spat into my face. "But I want you to know this isn't the last time you will see me."

Chapter Nine

Leaving the spectacle of cops and lights, I walked away speedily. I kept looking back over my shoulder as I walked, and every time I looked back, the cop was there watching me. I turned down the first block available, just to get out of the cop's glaring stare. As soon as I turned the corner, I broke out in a run. After ten blocks, I was tired and breathing heavy. I was confused as to why I had been let go and not my friends. I quickly chalked it up to my age.

I was too far away from my mother's home to make it all the way back on foot. There was no way I was going to call her to come pick me up either. Fortunately, my aunt only lived about six miles away. I ran and walked the entire distance, and it took me most of the night. When I arrived at my aunt's apartment, it was four in the morning. I timidly knocked on the door. After a few moments, my aunt opened her door with her robe pulled tight. Upon seeing me standing there, my forehead dotted with sweat, my clothing dirty and ragged, her mouth dropped. Her hands flew up to her mouth to cover the opening. She stared at me in disbelief.

"Kenyatta!" she exclaimed, finally. "Boy, where have you been? Your mother has been looking all over for you!" She grabbed me by the shoulder and pulled me in the house as if I might run away.

Inside, I sat down on the couch. My aunt sat beside me and grabbed the cordless phone from its cradle. She sat close to me. She

76

really thought that I might bolt and run away at any second. In an instant, I could hear my mother on the other line. I heard her voice raise an octave, and one second later, the conversation was over.

My aunt looked at me and said, "Your mom is on her way."

I was relieved to know that she was on the way. I hadn't seen her in weeks. My aunt told me to follow her into the dining room, and we sat at the dining room table. She poured me orange juice while we waited for my mom to show up. She sat down at the other end of the table.

"Are you okay, Ken?" she asked.

Her brow was wrinkled with concern. I could only imagine what she had heard. I nodded that I was good. I really didn't know what to say or how to say anything. I thought about L and Levi. I wondered if they had been let go. A part of me almost wanted to have gone to jail too, just to remain a part of what we had started.

It seemed like less than five minutes before I heard a heavy banging on the front door. My aunt stood up and crossed the room. My heart began to beat fast. I was almost more fearful of seeing my mom face to face than I had been during the high speed police chase. Then she was standing directly over me. I didn't know whether to duck or hug her.

"Stand up boy!" she said sternly.

I stood up with my head down. I couldn't look her in the eye. Then she hugged me long and hard. She cried. When she finally released me, we all sat down at the dining table.

"Where have you been, Kenyatta?" my mom asked. Before I had a chance to answer, she continued. "Do you know how worried your sisters, your grandparents, and I have been about you?"

I didn't have any answers.

"What have you been doing?" she asked. "We have been hearing things about you in the neighborhood. I pray to God that not one of the rumors I have heard about you is true. I didn't raise you to be any of those things."

I sat in despondency.

"Do you want to end up like your father?" she asked. The room was silent while she and my aunt waited for me to answer.

I finally looked up at her. "No," I answered.

I went home with my mother that morning. She made it clear that I would wake up and put on my clothes and go to school the very next day.

When I got to school, I was welcomed back like a celebrity. All the kids knew or had heard about the many things I had been involved in over the last month. Most of them were extreme fabrications. I never challenged or disputed any of the stories though. I welcomed the attention.

I attended church that weekend. My mom had been keeping close tabs on me. I met up with my old friend Josh while I was there, he told me how he was planning on becoming a lawyer one day. Then he asked me if I still had dreams of being a wide receiver. That was something I hadn't thought about in a long while.

I returned to school the next Monday. It was during my second period class that I heard my name called over the PA system. I was being called to the front office. When I got there, I could see the police and the principal through the glass. I thought to keep walking and leave, but I hadn't done anything, I assumed.

When I got inside, a uniformed officer asked, "Are you Kenyatta?"

Reluctantly, I answered, "Yes."

"Turn around and put your hands behind your back," the officer said.

I was confused. I hadn't done anything. Maybe they had made a mistake in letting me go before, I thought. My mind immediately recalled my mother asking me if I wanted to be like my father. As I was being escorted down the hall towards the exit, flanked by two police officers, the answer became obvious to me. It was too late, I was already like my father.

I sat on a gray concrete bench in the holding tank of the local jail, staring at the drab white walls. I assumed that at some point my mother would be there to pick me up. It didn't happen. A court's clerk and a correctional officer appeared at the holding tanks doors. They spoke to me through the small pane of Plexiglas. They told me that I was being held on a probation violation for truancy. Several hours later, I was in the back of a van being transported to the juvenile. It was clear by then that I wouldn't be going home that day.

The van pulled up to a set of great barbed wire gates. They pulled apart slowly, allowing the van entrance. The van pulled in and was stopped again by another set of barbed wire gates, fencing it in. The gates closed slowly behind us. The officer driving was on his radio often as we waited for the gates to close. I watched through the wire mesh glass of the van's windows as a correctional officer searched under the vehicle with a mirror. The gates behind us closed with a great jolt. I knew at that point it would take great risk to try to escape. I was locked up now. More gates opened in front of us and the van made its way around a compact concrete one-story structure. We drove up to a side door and the driver jumped out and let me out the side door of the van. I hobbled out off balance due to the leg shackles that had been locked around my ankles. I shuffled towards the building's double glass doors.

I stayed in juvenile hall for a week and a half, and it didn't feel so bad. I knew that I would be getting out soon, so I never was stressed. I knew about, or had met, most of the guys in there. We were peers. We told stories about all that we had done on the streets, and I had plenty to share. I had better stories because my hanging partners had been grown men. The others mostly told lies. I played basketball and watched TV the bulk of my short stay. Then, one day, I heard music to my ears. "Kenyatta Martin," a C.O. called, walking into the day room where I was watching TV. Instinctively, I knew that it was time for me to go, and I was ready.

"Pack it up!" the C.O said. That was the code for pack your belongings.

I quickly got up and went to my cell. I didn't have much. I stripped the sheets from the thin mattress, grabbed my shoes, and left. I tossed the sheets into the hall outside the cell and followed the C.O. out of the cell block. In the release tank, I was given my own clothing back, and an hour later I was let out of the tank and led through a side door where I was free once again.

To my surprise, my grandfather was standing on the other side of the door. He walked up to me and put his arm around my shoulder and walked me to his van. We got in the van in silence. Once he had started the van and pulled off the property of the juvenile he finally spoke. "So, how have you been?" he wanted to know.

Once we hit the highway, I knew we weren't headed to my mother's house. We were headed towards Tifton.

Chapter Ten

I slept the entire drive back. I was exhausted. The fact that I was headed back to Tifton was something I didn't know how to explain. I was looking forward to seeing my cousins, my old friends, and my grandmother. I couldn't wait to see what Warren had been up to. I woke up to the sounds of gravel grinding under the van's tires, and I knew that we had made it back to Tifton. I woke up and peered out the window at the house where I had spent most of my young life. The sun was beginning to set, and I could clearly recall the night we left. I envisioned the gun that was in my mother's lap and the first apartment we moved into when we first got to Atlanta.

When I got out of the car, Brian was the first one to burst through the screen door. He ran up on me swiftly, throwing playful jabs in my direction. "You forgot how to fight, Ken?" he jibed.

Germ was the next to come out the house. In a moment, I was boxing with both them in the front yard of my grandmother's house as if I had never left.

"Don't use up too much energy," my grandfather said as he headed into the house.

"Y'all still need to cut that grass," he added, letting the screen door slam behind him.

After a few moments of roughhousing, we ventured into the house.

I could smell the tantalizing aroma of freshly baked biscuits. I made a beeline for the kitchen. My grandmother was standing at the stove with her back to me. She turned around as if she had been waiting for me. When I looked her in her eyes, I saw that she was concerned. She pulled me close and held me close to her bosom.

"Kenyatta, my baby," she sang before kissing me on the cheek. Then she held me away and looked me square in the face. "I'm disappointed in you," she said. "Now sit down at that table and tell me your plans for fixing yourself now that you back home."

I sat down at the kitchen table. But before I could speak I saw a bag of plain potato chips on the kitchen counter. I grabbed the chips and poured some onto a paper towel. I picked up the hot sauce sitting in the center of the table with the other condiments. I hadn't had the combination of hot sauce and potato chips since I had left.

I spent the next thirty minutes eating chips and telling my grandmother my plans for going to school, playing football again, and, more importantly, staying out of trouble. I felt relieved like I had left all the indelible things I had done back in Atlanta. The two years I had spent in Atlanta soon began to feel like I had only been away on a summer vacation.

I quickly found my stride back in Tifton. I started school almost immediately. Warren and I were soon back to our old antics, terrorizing other neighborhoods, playing a lot of football, and being kids. Sometimes I would think about L, Levi, Rocco, and Jennifer. I hadn't heard from them and knew it was a good possibility that I would never even see them again. People at my school in Tifton had missed me, and stories of some of my wild exploits in Atlanta had made it all the way back there.

It didn't take long for me to fall in love either. There was a girl in my third period class who I was very much attracted to. She was one of the better-known girls in the school, mainly she because she looked like the singer Aaliyah, a renowned R&B artist out at the time. Her name was Penny. She was light complexioned with a slim figure and dark bangs that covered one side of her face.

It took a couple days, but soon Penny began to like me too. I was different because of my experiences in Atlanta. The entire school respected me because of my reputation for being a bad boy. I'm sure she found this attractive. Everything was looking up now. I began to realize that, although I thought I was having fun in Atlanta, it was a lot more appealing to be able to move about without having to look over my shoulder for the police. I joined the school's football team and began to showcase my skills once more. In just two weeks' time, my entire life had changed.

Two days into my third week back in Tifton, my grandfather called me outside to the backyard. We walked a few yards from the house, and he stopped near a tree stump. He propped his foot up on the stump. I picked up a stick out of nervousness and I swung it at the air while I waited for him to talk; the seriousness of what he had to say was unmistakable.

"I got a call from your mother," he began. "She says that the police have been by her house. Detectives too. It seems as if they are looking for you about some armed robberies."

I looked down at the ground and drew my name in the dirt with the stick.

"Kenyatta, look at me, boy," my grandfather said.

I looked him in the eye.

"Did you have anything to do with those robberies, son?" he asked.

I saw every robbery I had ever been a part of run through my mind at that moment. But I shook my head no.

"I don't know what they talking about, Granddad," I replied slowly.

He stepped off the stump, walked up to me, and put a hand on my shoulder.

"The police are looking for you," he said as a matter of fact. "If and when they do show up to question you, you don't tell them anything until I get there."

I looked away and down at the ground. He lifted my head back up.

"Don't tell them police nothing, Kenyatta. You wait until I show up. Do you understand, son?" he asked sternly.

I nodded yes. "I understand," I answered.

He shook his head a little, clearly grieved. Then he turned and headed for the house.

I stood, watching him walk away. The police were looking for me. I wasn't scared though. Talking to the police and going to jail was all quickly becoming a normal part of life. I was thirteen, I hadn't been taught anything other than what I had seen or learned from those around me. That faulty education was quickly catching up with me.

"Yo, Ken!" a voice called, snatching me from my daydream. It was Warren.

"Let's go, boy, they picking teams over on the Eastside," he called from the edge of the street.

I dropped the stick and ran towards him. When I caught up, we both ran to the Eastside to play football.

Two days after the conversation with my grandfather in the backyard, I was sitting in class. It was almost lunch time, I kept watching the clock tick by because I was looking forward to my lunch date with Penny. I had quickly forgotten about Levi's sister, Jennifer, after I had met Penny. I had football practice after lunch. The day was certainly looking up again.

Right before the period was about to end, the principal walked into the classroom. He walked up to my teacher and leaned down and whispered into her ear. I watched as her eyes shot directly to me.

"Kenyatta, can you come up here, please?" she called out quickly.

I stood up from my desk and approached the head of the class.

"Kenyatta," the principal said to me in a hushed tone, "I need you to come with me. You have visitors."

My stomach churned vigorously. I followed the principal out of the class and into the hallway, where two uniformed officers were waiting. I immediately recognized one of the officers standing there. It was the exact same police officer who had let me go the night Levi and Rocco had gotten locked up after the high-speed chase. He smiled wide as he saw the recognition dance in my eyes.

"Mr. Martin," he said, "I told you I would see you again, didn't I?"

I didn't answer. I remembered that my grandfather had told me not to talk to them. I walked with them to the principal's office. They questioned me about the robberies of the two men in the Cadillac and the shootings on Buford Highway. Essentially, they knew everything. I didn't quite understand why they were asking me questions if they already knew the answers. I tried to stall; I asked to speak with my grandfather, and they told me that he was already on the way. They said that if I wanted to leave with him when he did arrive, I had better cooperate.

They asked me a million questions in the small confines of that

87

office. The three white men glared at me from all angles as if I was an animal at the zoo. All of them dominant authority figures, I never stood a chance. They persisted with their interrogation. I wanted to tell them what they wanted to hear so that I could leave. I reasoned that if I just told them what happened, I still would have time to at least catch football practice. I had already missed my date with Penny.

So, I began to talk. I told them everything I could about anything they asked. They recorded the conversation and jotted down notes on paper. I signed some papers after that, then they told me to stand up at that time. I did. I thought that my grandfather would be showing up to take me home at any moment. Then the officer who had promised to see me again said, "Put your hands behind your back."

I put my hands behind my back, and for the second time in less than a month I was headed back to jail. Outside the school was a transport van, equipped with wire meshed windows. They helped me up into the van and, just as simply as I had left, I was now headed back to Atlanta. I had charges to face. There was no truth to my being able to go home for assisting them as they had promised. It had all been a lie. The officers did stop at a McDonald's, though. They bought me a Big Mac and a vanilla ice cream cone. They took the cuffs off and let me enjoy the meal from the back of the van. I ate and when I was done, they put the cuffs back around my wrists. I settled into the stiff vinyl seating and prepared for the long ride back to Atlanta. The last thing I thought before I nodded off was, *At least I might be able to see Levi, L or Rocco.*

Chapter Eleven

It felt like I had only been asleep a few minutes before I heard the officers issuing commands over their CB radios. I knew we were in front of some form of jail. I opened my eyes and saw that we were at the same juvenile I had left only one month before. They helped me out the rear of the van, and I was taken inside. When I went in, the staff recognized me. I was properly booked in and assigned a cell. This time they issued me an orange jumpsuit and, again, the only thing I could keep was my sneakers. I grabbed my thin mattress, my small bag of toiletries, and headed into the pod towards my cell. As I passed through the day room, I recognized some of the same faces from before. Then I recognized a face I hadn't seen in what seemed like an eternity. Sitting in front of the TV was Levi.

I dropped my mattress and yelled his name aloud.

"Yo, Levi!"

He turned around and recognized me instantly. In a moment, he was out his seat and we slapped hands in the middle of the room. It was a weird reunion. So many unanswered questions. He helped me put my things in my cell. Then we found a space in the day room and we talked. He told me that Rocco and L were being held in the county jail. Because of their ages, they were being charged as adults. He explained that he was being charged with several counts of armed robbery and about eight aggravated assaults.

89

He enlightened me as to the events that led up to our being ambushed by the police. Turned out, it was Lisa's parents who had called the police. They had been looking for her while she had been staying with us. Not only that, they were already upset that she was now dating a black guy. They had watched the news and recognized the Caprice, Levi, and L. They were the ones who tipped the police off. The parents had even allowed the police to tap their phones. The police had also staked out Lisa's home. When L had taken her home that day, he was promptly arrested. This was the reason why he had never made it back to the mansion.

I was floored. I had no idea that all those things had taken place. Interestingly enough, it all made sense.

It didn't take long for Levi and me to reunite as best friends. We were back to having each other's backs inside the juvenile. On my third day in, I was called to the nurse's office to get a physical. I was also given an STD test. Two days later, I was called back into the nurse's office for the results. I sat down in a metal folding chair in the corner of the small nurse's office. The nurse was a slim white woman with square-rimmed glasses. She read my name from a clipboard in her hand. She looked up over the rim of her glasses at me for clarification. I nodded.

The nurse turned towards the small sink and pulled on two latex gloves.

"You have gonorrhea," she said while she fished around in a drawer next to her.

She pulled a vacuum-sealed syringe from the drawer. "I need you to drop your pants," she said smoothly. "I have to give you a shot in the rear," she said while plucking the body of the syringe lightly.

I nervously pulled down the trousers of my uniform. As she gave me the shot, I remembered Bonnie. She was the only one I had had intercourse with ever. I knew it was from her that I had contracted the STD. I was just happy that I hadn't caught anything deadly.

I received my first court date before the week ended. Again, I was handcuffed and shackled. On this morning, I was not alone on the bus. I was handcuffed with another one of the juvenile's inmates. His name was Shark. I knew Shark from inside juvenile hall but he stayed to himself. He would only talk when he played pool. Then you couldn't shut him up at any time. In the van, during the ride to the courthouse, he told me that he was going to court for a murder charge. He was alleged to have killed his cousin during a dice game. He was fourteen years old. I told him I had armed robbery charges. As young as we were, we were both being charged as adults.

In the court's building, they kept me and Shark separated from the adults in our own holding tank. When it was my turn to go into the courtroom, they removed my handcuffs, and armed officers escorted me down a hallway and into the courtroom. The courtroom was cold and quiet. The judge and lawyers in the room had their heads down. They were busy with paperwork when I entered and sat down on the benches in front of the judge. A short while after that, the bailiff called my name. I nervously walked to the front of the court, not sure of where to stand. The bailiff pointed to the right of me. I stood behind a table next to a big gut white man in a mismatched suit.

He whispered in my ear, "I'll be representing you. Plead not guilty when the judge asks you how you plead."

I nodded, and when the judge asked me how I was pleading, I pled not guilty.

That was all that happened that day. I was escorted out of the courtroom and into the hallway where I was handcuffed again and told to wait with my back up against the wall. A moment later, the lawyer from the courtroom appeared and introduced himself. He said he was my public defender, he was assigned to assist me throughout the case. I was indifferent towards him. I detected no sincerity in his speech.

I left the courtroom that day just as confused about my future as I had been before I went inside. I met up with Shark in the holding tank. He was a tall, dark-skinned guy with matted hair. They called him Shark because of how he looked. His mouth was as wide as a shark's. When I came in the cell, he was standing in the middle of the room rapping songs. "What it look like?" I asked him as the metal door slammed shut behind me.

"Them crackers still trying to give me life," he said nonchalantly.

I told him that I had pled not guilty. Shark then began to enlighten me about the seven deadly sin laws. He had already been in juvenile for seven months before I had gotten there, so he was versed in some of the laws affecting his case. His case was high profile because it was a murder case. He had already known about the new law that stated juveniles between the ages of thirteen and seventeen could be tried as adults if they had committed any of the seven deadly sins. Murder and armed robbery were both on the list.

Shark wasn't optimistic at all about what could be the outcome of his case. He listed the reasons. One was his court appointed attorney, and the other was the law.

"I'm just ready to get to Alto," he said.

"What's Alto?" I asked.

"Where they send everybody convicted of a violent crime under seventeen years old," he said, walking over to the cell door and peering out into the hall from the small pane of Plexiglas. He threw up his boxing set and started throwing jabs at the door.

"You gotta be ready to throw them thangs in Alto," he said with animation while he mixed it up with the door.

Shark was ready to do his time. He wasn't concerned with fighting for his freedom. He felt like he was doomed anyway. I didn't know if that was how I was supposed to feel. I didn't want to go to Alto. I wanted to go back to Tifton, see my girlfriend Penny, and play football with Warren.

The cell door opened, and officers placed Shark and me in handcuffs and ankle shackles. Then we were taken back to the juvenile.

That next weekend, I got my first visitation. My mother and my oldest sister Pam came to the juvenile. My name was called over the intercom, and a correctional officer escorted me from my cell to the visitation room. I could see my mom and sister sitting in a circle made up of three chairs. I was buzzed into the visitation room, and I walked up to my mother and sister. I was genuinely happy to see them. We hugged and we sat down to talk.

"So how you doing, Kenyatta?" my mom asked.

"I'm OK. Ready to get out," I said.

"I know you are," she said as a matter of fact. "I'm ready for you to get out too. I spoke with your public defender. The court is offering you thirty years." She shook her head solemnly. "I'm going to have to get you a lawyer."

The number thirty bounced around in my head. I didn't know how to process thirty years, I was only thirteen years old.

"I told him that he and the court were retarded if they think I would allow you to take thirty years!" my mom continued. She put her hand on my leg to comfort me. "I get my income taxes back in a few months. I'm going to get you a paid lawyer."

I began to shake uncontrollably while she talked. My nose began to run. My sister noticed first.

"You OK, Kenyatta?" she asked.

I had been having shaking moments for the past week, but no one else had addressed it.

My mom eyed me for a moment and shook her head. "Those are withdrawal symptoms, Pam," she said to my sister.

"I know those signs all too well," she explained. "It's OK, Son," she continued. "We going to make it through this. But while you're in here I want you to think about all the things I used to tell you. Things like get up and get ready for school, Ken, or stop staying out late, Ken. Now, look around you. You still have to do those exact things."

She had made a good point.

We spent the rest of the hour talking about the rest of the family and how much they missed me. Then, just before my mom was about to leave, she told me about a man she had met. Her face lit up when she spoke about him. She said that he had changed her life and that she couldn't wait for me to meet him. She looked genuinely happy, and that made me feel good. Someone else could protect her until I got home.

After my first court date, every time after that, I always went to court with Levi. He had more charges than me though. He had multiple aggravated assault charges for his many drive-by shootings. The most damaging evidence that the state had against me were my own statements. I should have listened to my grandfather when he told me not to talk to the police about my case. I hadn't listened, and now these were the exact words the prosecutor was trying to use to hang me.

Chapter Twelve

We had been to court three separate times in three months, and the justice system was still offering me thirty years. Levi and I would sit in the day room and talk about our cases. We had different lawyers, but a few of our cases overlapped. As it stood, we were both on the verge of going to trial. I would sometimes lie in my bunk and stare at the ceiling through the night and into the early morning. I was positive that there would be a trial because there was no way I would plead out to thirty years. It was hard to sleep. I was thirteen. My life hadn't even begun, and they were trying to take it away.

The pressures of the case were beginning to affect my attitude. I was bumping heads with other inmates daily. One day, I was in my cell waiting my turn to come out to take a shower. I was pacing and occasionally looking out the small rectangle glass on my cell room door out into the hallway. We weren't allowed to take our shoes inside the cells, so we kept them in the hall in front of our cell door. I had the latest Charles Barkley basketball sneakers. They were crisp and new. Since my mother had begun to date her new boyfriend, she was able to provide me with whatever I wanted while I was locked away. As I stared out into the hallway, I saw another inmate walk by my room and intentionally kick my shoes out of place.

I immediately banged on the door.

"Hey homey!" I yelled out into the hall from behind the heavy metal door of my cell.

He never stopped to acknowledge me.

I yelled out into the hall again, "Nigga! If you don't fix my damn shoes, we going to have a problem when I come out!" I threatened.

The inmate stopped in his tracks and turned back around to look at me. He walked up to my cell door and stared me in the face through the glass.

"Bitch! You ain't gon do shit!" he growled before walking off towards the showers.

I was furious. I knew that if we were ever in the same room at the same time, there would be a fight. I was angry that I was locked up then. I was angry that I was facing thirty years. I was angry that he had disrespected me.

"When the doors swing, you swing!" I yelled out the door as he disappeared down the hall.

A short moment later, my door unlocked. It was my turn to take a shower. I came out in only my boxer shorts with a towel draped over my shoulders, but I had no intention of taking a shower. I came out the cell and took off my shower shoes. I quickly put on my sneakers. The corrections officer was preoccupied handing out bars of soap to the line of inmates waiting their turn for the shower. I ran down the hall up to where the guy who had kicked my shoes was standing in line. As I took off down the hall, the CO screamed out, "Hey! Inmate Martin! Stop!"

This alerted my target to my presence. He turned around just as I met him with a right cross. We began to fight in the cramped quarters of the hallway. We only had a few seconds to mix it up before the COs got involved and pulled us apart. I was handcuffed and dragged back to my cell. They removed my cuffs and pushed me into my room. I paced the small confines of the room with my anger boiling over. I didn't know what had me more infuriated, the fact that my shoes had been kicked down the hall or just the number thirty.

After that fight, the tone was set for the months that followed. The longer I was confined, and after every court appearance, the more the words Shark had said to me in the holding tank began to ring true. I felt like I was in a no-win situation. The magnitude of the crimes I was being accused of sounded and felt more dangerous and violent than when I had committed them. The prosecutor would never deviate from his offer of thirty years.

My mother and her boyfriend eventually got me a paid lawyer, and I finally had someone on my side who was fighting back. He made me feel comfortable about how we would approach the case.

My lawyer was a slim, white male with sandy-brown hair. He was young and quick-witted. He had sympathy for me because of my age. Based on my story, he understood exactly how I had ended up in the situation I was in now. That wasn't enough to stop me from lashing out from behind the confines of the juvenile walls. I fought with other inmates once a week and was in confinement three times out of every week just for fighting. Levi and I had each other's backs though. If one of us fought, then we both fought.

One day, my lawyer showed up at the juvenile unannounced. He and I sat alone in the recreation room at one of the lunch tables that evening. He sat across from me and told me that I had a trial date set and that we would be picking a jury the next week. He told me that we had a good shot at getting the charges reduced. I wanted to be optimistic, but I hadn't any reason to at that point. Reduced charges weren't spelling freedom.

That night, I was sleeping in my cell when I heard a soft tap on my cell door. I sat up and saw Shark at the door, grinning broadly. He had gotten forty years for the murder of his cousin just two weeks earlier. I got up and walked to the door.

"I'm out, homey!" Shark said, smiling, all his teeth showing. "On my way to Alto," he said as if he was headed off to college.

He stepped back from the door so that I could see his entire body. He began to throw blows into the air.

"You gotta be ready to throw them hands, Ken!" he yelled, his voice echoing in the silent hall.

An officer called for Shark to move on from where he was standing.

"I'll see you on the other side, Ken," Shark said. "Unless them crackers let you go. Good luck, bro," he added, throwing up the deuces before disappearing down the hall. I hoped I would never see him again, but it was looking like I was right behind him.

The next week, I was handcuffed, shackled, and taken to the courthouse. In the holding tank, an officer brought in a suit that my mother had bought. I had to wear civilian clothes while I picked my jury. My lawyer spent close to seven hours interviewing potential jurors. I was not impressed by any juror that came through the interview process. They were all old white men and women, and most, if any, never bothered to look me in my eye.

I went back to the juvenile that evening and I told Levi about the jury. He said that he was going to plead out because of all the evidence they had against him. He was facing a lot more time than I was, so he couldn't risk it.

The day before my trial date I didn't eat at all. The night before my trial, I didn't sleep at all. I was handcuffed, shackled, and taken to the courthouse. In the holding tank, I dressed in my suit once again. I was cuffed and escorted to the courtroom. Before I went in, my handcuffs were removed. I went into the courtroom and saw my mother and her new boyfriend seated on the benches at the back of the room. Right after that, I looked at the jury. It was all white, except for one elderly black man. I knew for certain that Shark had been correct about all that he had prophesied. Thirty minutes later, the trial began.

The prosecutor was a white male with a pudgy, red face and a bad

101

toupee. He began his opening argument and immediately had the jury eating from his hands. It looked as if he was friends with the jurors. There was jovial body language. The jurors appeared to be overly receptive to his words. The prosecutor labeled me a threat to society. He promised the jury that he would prove that I held the victims against their will, at gunpoint, while stripping them of their belongings, thereby committing the crime of armed robbery. By the time the prosecutor had concluded his opening arguments I could feel intense glares coming from the jury booth.

Then it was my lawyer's turn. The jurors listened closely as he explained that there was no real evidence, only hearsay; that there was no concrete proof that could put me in, or around, any of the events that led up to my being arrested and charged with armed robbery. He also explained that he would prove beyond a reasonable doubt that I did not commit an armed robbery, that I did not possess a weapon, and that I was a victim of circumstance, a child who was being manipulated by adult criminals to assist them in their exploits. When he was finished speaking, I felt a little better. Maybe I did have a chance. My lawyer was certainly working for his paycheck.

During the afternoon session, the victims were called to the stand. The two white men I had robbed took the stand one at a time. During both interrogations by the prosecutor, they were asked if I was indeed the culprit who had brandished a gun and robbed them of all their personal belongings. Neither of the two victims could positively identify me as being the perpetrator. Next, the arresting cops were called to the stand. Things took a turn for the worse. They read my own statements aloud in the courtroom. I basically had given them the entire conviction on a silver platter in that principal's office back in Tifton. The prosecutor did not have to prove I had done anything. I had already confessed.

My mom took the stand. She told the judge and the jurors that I had a promising football career ahead of me. She said I was a good kid who deserved a chance at life. She wanted the jurors to know that I was a victim more than a hardened criminal. She was the perfect character witness.

My lawyer followed my mother's testimony up with his closing arguments. In his seventeen-minute speech, he summed up the case. He told the jury that had I not lived in the neighborhood I had lived in, if I had not been born a black male and exposed to all the corruption that most low-income black males are exposed to, then I would not have even been in the courtroom that day. He testified that if I had been born the son of a politician, or the son of a doctor, the court would have seen fit to seek rehabilitation efforts other than that of prison. My lawyer spoke the truth, and I was proud. The jury deliberated and, in two hours, they came back with a verdict.

Chapter Thirteen

I sat in the holding tank with my elbows resting on my knees, my face planted in the palm of my hands. I had been pacing the small holding cell for two hours while the jury deliberated. The entire time I waited I could only think about Shark's philosophies. I knew I was Alto bound. I grew up fighting, so, if it came to it I would and could fight. I still feared the notion of going to Alto State Prison though. The stories I heard from others in the juvenile, even from some of the COs, were not for the faint of heart.

I knew I would miss my mother when I was sent away. She was doing better than I had ever seen her do in my life, and she was happy. She was in love, and her significant other appeared to be successful. I wanted to be around her while she was happy. It seemed that in the few short months that I had been gone so much had changed about me. I used to avoid being around my family members, now I missed them and wanted to be a part of the things they had going on in their lives.

The door of the holding tank buzzed open, and my lawyer stood at the door. "The jury has reached a verdict," he said blandly.

Even he felt like Shark. I could tell that by his closing arguments. The justice system was not fair. He put his hand on my shoulder as we walked back to the courtroom.

Inside, I sat down at the defendant's table. All the while I was shaking like I was facing the electric chair. It wasn't because of withdrawals that I was shaking, it was pure nervousness. The jury filed in and took their places in the jury box. Once they were seated, the judge spoke.

"Has the jury reached a decision?" he asked.

A frail, elderly, white female juror stood and read from the paper in her hand.

"For count one of armed robbery, we the jury find the defendant not guilty."

My eyes widened a little. Maybe Shark hadn't known what he was talking about, I reasoned.

"To the charges of aggravated assault, we the jury find the defendant not guilty," the juror continued. "For the final account of the armed robbery, we the jury, find the defendant guilty," she said before finding her seat.

I heard my mom gasp in the rear of the room. I was slightly confused. I had been found not guilty and guilty? The judge acknowledged the jury's findings and then set a sentencing court date for the next week. I was escorted from the courtroom. My lawyer met me at the holding tank. He came into the tank with me and sat on the concrete bench beside me.

"I'm sorry we couldn't get all the charges tossed," he said. "The good news is you aren't looking at the thirty years anymore. But armed robbery carries a mandatory minimum of ten years. At the least, you're looking at ten years. You'll be twenty-three when you get out."

I stared down at the drab, gray concrete floor, my head hanging down in despondency. I had nothing to say.

"You're only thirteen," my lawyer continued. "You'll still be young when you get out of jail. Just promise me to stay out of trouble and make it home to your mom," he added.

I nodded while still staring at the ground. I was sick to my stomach. It was hard to accept that I would be gone for ten years. In fact, I didn't accept it. I held on to hope, trusting that at the sentencing I would be shown leniency based on my age and other circumstances.

The week before sentencing flew by quickly. I did a lot of sleeping and thinking that week, and before I was aware of it, I was standing in the courtroom once again. The judge never looked at me. He asked the prosecutor for their sentencing guidelines and recommendations. Then I was sentenced to the mandatory minimum sentence of ten years. It was official, I would not see daylight again until I was twenty-three years old. Just like that, I was escorted out of the courtroom and back to the holding tanks. I saw my mother in my peripheral view. She was crying profusely with her boyfriend cradling her in his arms.

I wanted to make a quick break for the exit door in a last attempt to avoid prison, but I couldn't build up the courage. I hated to see my mom cry. For the first time in my short life on Earth I realized I had hurt other people with my actions, not just myself. This was a lesson that would haunt me all the days of my prison life.

Levi got sentenced to twenty years for his crimes a few weeks after me. Only days after his sentencing, I got the early morning wake-up call at my cell door. The correctional officer opened my cell door wide.

"Kenyatta Martin! Pack it up! You're going to Alto!" he said before slamming the door shut.

I lay in the bunk for a moment. For three weeks I had been preparing myself for this trip. Now that the time had come for me to go, I was ready mentally and physically. I let my feet hit the cold concrete floor and I began to gather my few belongings. When I had packed up my things, I made a quick stop at Levi's cell; I hollered through the crack in his door to wake him up right then. I told him I would see him in Alto. He threw up the peace sign, and I left.

I was escorted to a holding area in the juvenile. There I was shackled and handcuffed. I was taken by van to the county jail where I was transferred to a bus with other prisoners. We had all been found guilty of a crime and sentenced to hard time. I sat at the front of the bus and was relatively quiet during the bus trip. I had a lot on my mind. I made it a point to stay up and watch the scenery in the hopes that I could remember a route back to my city. The other inmates chatted throughout the early morning, most of them discussing how much time they had. Other, seasoned, penitentiary vets were already crossing their fingers in hopes they would get sent to the prison of their choice. Obviously, for a lot of the men, this wasn't their first bus trip to prison.

There was one guy sitting right behind me on the bus. I had looked him in his eye when I first sat down there. You could tell by his muscle bound build that he had spent most of his jail time working out. He was the loudest talker on the bus. He talked about how many people he had knocked out with his hand game. He spoke this way the entire three-hour bus ride. In fact, he was our entertainment for the whole ride.

When we finally pulled up to the prison, we could barely see the great brick compound hidden behind all the barbed wire gates that surrounded the building. There were gun towers with armed correctional officers who peered down from great heights watching everybody and everything. We drove through three sets of parted barbed wire gates and parked. The prison itself looked like an ancient vampire's castle. Quickly, Alto was living up to its reputation.

"Welcome to Alto!" the bus driver said as he killed the bus's engine.

"What we doing at Alto?" I heard the guy sitting behind me say aloud.

Everyone on the bus immediately noticed his change in tone. He wasn't as loud and boisterous when he spoke.

"This is your new home," the bus driver joked as he exited the bus.

108

Another correctional officer got on the bus and opened the cage behind which we sat. We hobbled off one by one, the ankle shackles tightening with every movement. We were made to stand in line. I was one of the first people off. As I stood to wait for our next instructions, I heard the CO yelling at an inmate to get off the bus, then there was scuffling. I could hear the muscle bound guy who had been sitting behind me yelling, refusing to get off the bus.

"I didn't know I was coming to Alto!" he screamed. He was consumed with fear.

In a short moment, the prison certified response team appeared, dressed in all black fatigues. I had never seen white men, or any men at all, the size of these men before in my life. They looked like they had just run off the football field.

The CERT team pulled the guy off the bus kicking and screaming. You would have thought they were taking him to the gas chamber. I never saw him again. I had only heard that he had been signed into protective custody. I couldn't believe that a grown man could be that scared. I wasn't scared, but what I did learn by watching him get pulled off the bus was that it was real in here.

We were lined up and escorted into the prison. We had to walk with our shoulders touching the wall and stop and stand at attention if anyone of importance passed us in the hallway. The white vinyl prison floors were buffed to a high shine. Inmates in white state uniforms with blue stripes milled about the halls of the prison, involved in various aspects of detailing the building. Some mopped, others buffed the floors, and others cleaned the windows. The prison was its own community. It was the strictest place I had ever been.

We were taken to an open spaced locker room equipped with long wooden benches. We lined up in front of the benches and our handcuffs and shackles were removed. We were made to strip naked before being searched. Next, we were made to shower with potent lice shampoo and soap. Then a barber shaved our heads clean. We were given a mattress, sheets, and a Ziploc bag filled with toiletries. After that, we were assigned cell blocks. By the time the entire intake process was done, it was two p.m., and I was sleeping on my feet. I was readily anticipating getting to the cell block.

Two others and I were called out of the group; we were the youngest. We were going across the yard to where the juveniles were housed, and, infamously, the most dangerous part of the entire prison. I was ready though.

The juvenile housing pod did not disappoint. When I stepped into the shiny floored pod, the first thing I noticed was that the floor was littered with batteries, all sizes and types. I looked up an inmate was yelling at me from the second tier of the pod.

"Pick up as many of those batteries as you can and hold um," he commanded from his post.

You could feel the tension in the air. Something was taking place, and I had walked right into the midst of it. I had a decision to make, something told me it would be to my benefit to pick the batteries up. I picked up a handful and carried my belongings on into my cell. My roommate was standing in the cell with two handfuls of batteries himself. He was a short, light-skinned guy, wearing a black wave cap tied onto his head. He was dressed in a white T-shirt and multiple pairs of white boxer shorts that he wore like real shorts. "What's up my nigga?" he asked when I came in.

"What's up?" I replied, slamming my mattress onto the top bunk.

He walked over to the cell door covertly. A loud buzz echoed, the pod's main entrance door was opened, and an officer came in the building. Immediately, he was pelted with batteries until he retreated. I watched as my roommate screamed obscenities at the officer while throwing batteries at his head with force and speed. They were trying to hurt him. I could hear the batteries landing and pinging off the walls and floors.

"Faggot ass COs won't let us get a rec, and they trying to keep us locked up in these rooms about some shit ain't got nothing to do with us!" my roommate explained out loud, more to himself than me.

"What's your name, bro?" he asked after he calmed a bit.

"My name Ken," I said. "What they call you?"

"My name is Kane," he said, just as the main door buzzed open again.

He crept up to the cell door like an assassin and again began hurling batteries from the cell at the officers who had come in. I had officially walked into a war zone.

Chapter Fourteen

From my very first day at Alto, the tone had been set for my prison campaign. Fights, stabbings, and murders were a way of life in Alto. People were getting their heads busted wide open with padlocks, mop ringers, and other objects. Since I was housed in the juvenile section of the prison, taking GED classes was mandatory. The first morning of my classes, I saw my roommate sharpening his pencil extra pointed. He tightened his shoes tight. Then he removed his wave cap and brushed his hair in the wavy reflection of the false mirror in our cell.

"Roll with me today," Kane said. "I'll show you how not to get shanked out here on the yard."

Shanked was a term that referred to being stabbed by a homemade blade of some sort. He left the cell, and I followed. He turned around immediately and stopped me in my tracks, pointing at my shoes. I had only planned to wear shower shoes to class.

"Nigga, where you going with them shower shoes on?" Kane asked. I looked down at my feet, confused.

"To GED class," I said.

He shook his head vigorously. "Nah bro, you gotta strap up," he replied.

"Strap up," was the term used for putting on your sneakers. This was an inmate's first line of defense in any altercation. If an inmate went to put his sneakers on, you knew that violence was soon to follow. The urgency in Kane's voice let me know I should heed his advice. I immediately put on my sneakers.

"Them some real-life wolves over there at the GED center," he went on to explain. "Them older dudes over there been locked up since before we were born, bro. They thirsty for some action. Young niggas get raped over there every day."

Kane seemed almost offended that I hadn't known the rules of the GED engagement. Before I left, I sharpened the edge of my pencil a little sharper.

True to his word, the older prisoners who were in the GED program did make passes at us. There were cat calls and crude propositions from the grown men. Us juveniles all stuck by one another's sides though. If one of us fought, all of us fought. That first day in GED class never ended or so it seemed. The war between us and the older men was ongoing and continuous. They never stopped trying to rape us, and we never stopped fighting for our lives.

It was during my six months in Alto that I began to catch my stride as an inmate. I had a clique of friends who had become my brothers. My mom and her boyfriend had been doing exceptionally well. I benefited greatly from her success. My locker box was always stocked with honey buns and ramen noodles. I had pajamas, house shoes, and the latest sneakers. Even though I was locked away, I felt blessed. There were many around me who had no family to provide for them while they did their bids.

After only six months in, my prison life took a catastrophic turn. My mother came to visit me one Saturday. Before I even entered the visitation room I knew something was wrong. She was uncomfortable; the smiles that she had worn throughout the previous visitations were noticeably absent.

"What's wrong, mah?" I asked while sliding into the plastic blue chair across from her.

There was a small plastic table between us. Neither of us could cross the table except at the beginning of visitation to hug and say hello and at the end of visitation to hug and say goodbye. On the table were a soda and a bag of chips. I opened the chips.

"There is something I need to tell you, Ken," she said somberly. I popped the top on my soda nonchalantly. "It's about my boyfriend. He is a drug dealer. We got caught with some drugs a while back when they raided our apartment."

She dropped her head. "I hated to tell you this, but I pled guilty and got an eighteen month sentence," she told me, fidgeting with her fingernails.

I stopped swallowing mid swallow and sat the drink bottle down on the table. I couldn't believe what I was hearing. I still didn't fully comprehend what she had said. It was hard to process that she was going to be doing time or the fact that she had been selling drugs. This was my mama speaking. The woman who had stressed the dangers of breaking the law. Things then began to make sense though. This explained how I had been so well taken care of all these months I had mixed emotions about what she was telling me. But life for me thus far had been extremely awkward and uncanny. Besides, I had no choice but to accept it.

I hugged her a little longer before she left that day. She had tears in her eyes. I didn't cry. I just returned to my dormitory confused. Prison life after that visitation was totally different. The commissary began to dissipate, the sneakers began to lean, and I even missed a few Christmas packages. Through it all, time still passed. There was even a point in time where at mail call I would receive letters from both my mother and father—the three of us all corresponding from separate prisons. My grandparents took time out of their lives to visit as much as they could the first three years of my prison sentence. The last time my grandfather came to visit, he was barely able to recognize me, he had Alzheimer's. He passed the next year.

My grandmother passed almost a year later. The loss of my grandparents really touched me. I hadn't cried through a lot of my adversities, but this was stronger than me. Again, I was forced to learn that your actions hurt others and that you could lose people along the way. All the times I had been robbing and selling drugs, I had never anticipated going to prison or losing relatives to death while locked away. I wasn't even allowed to attend the funerals of my grandfather or my grandmother.

The one thing that was on my side was time. I had been incarcerated during the most influential years of my life, yet I still had my entire life ahead of me. It was shortly after my grandmother passed that I began to want better for myself. I thought about my life and what I could do differently. I knew that at least I would be getting out one day. I did the math again. I would be twenty-three years old when I got out of prison. I knew that the first step to having a future when I got out was for me to at least have my GED. Although the GED classes were some of the most dangerous times of my incarceration, I began to take them seriously.

As I grew older, the threats from the older convicts became nil. The GED classes were where I also had the closest interaction with civilians. There were female teachers and tutors. Because I was so young, this was like a real school to me. I was in the GED classes for six out of my ten years incarcerated. At the age of seventeen, I was finally moved across the yard to the adult section of the prison. It was then that I began to build a relationship with one of the teachers. She was in her thirties. She was a white woman with short hair and a cute face. She was very much interested in me. She would make sure I ate well and had certain items that weren't allowed in the prison.

Between her and my cousin Brian, the loss of financial support from my mother had begun to offset itself. As I was nearing my release, Brian and I had built an even stronger bond. He used to send me pictures of all his cars, women, jewelry, and vacations. He was selling cocaine now, and he kept my commissary plentiful. He had found success as a dope boy. He was just as excited as I was when it came to my release date. He couldn't wait to show me his lifestyle outside of the still photos that he had been sending.

Nine years in prison had been treacherous, but I was young, so I hadn't left any responsibilities on the streets. So I could maintain better than most. In the adult section of the prison, men had to deal with wives and kids that they had left behind. I knew that doing time was harder for them. I'm sure it was because of this aspect that my bid passed as quickly as it did. Of course, it didn't feel like it was ever moving fast enough, until the last year.

It was during my last year that I was sent to a halfway house to finish out the last six months of my sentence. The halfway house was the closest thing to freedom I had experienced since the day I had been transported from Tifton back to Atlanta. Here, we could wear civilian clothes and work with the public. I quickly got a job at a bakery and was earning a paycheck.

Visitations were better in the halfway house. I could speak and visit with my family as if they were in my own living room. After three months in the halfway house, I was allowed to go out and visit with my family at my mother's house for several unsupervised hours before I had to return to the halfway house. The stage was set for me to get out of prison and be productive. I was mature, had a GED, and because I was making money and spending none, it was guaranteed that I was getting out with savings.

Then, just one month before I was to be released, my sister told me that my cousin Brian had been murdered. I became depressed. Although I was getting out, I still struggled with the loss of so many family members. Brian's death was only encouragement for me to stay on the straight and narrow course when I was released. Brian's murder had been drug related.

I sat on the edge of my bunk flipping through the many pictures he had sent me throughout my incarceration. The cars, the parties, the clothing, and the girls all seemed so insignificant now that he was gone. I wanted the memories of his death and of my parents' and my incarcerations to stay fresh in my mind. I vowed never to forget the consequences of living the fast life. Then I was released.

Chapter Fifteen

The first thing I did when I got out was report to my probation officer. I had five years' probation to complete. My sister Pam took me to her home where a multitude of my family and friends had gathered to celebrate my release. My childhood friend Josh and his mother even showed up to show their support. It was great seeing Josh. While I was away in prison, he had been away at Tennessee State attending college. As it stood, he was now on his way to Houston to finish up his law degree. Talking to Josh took me all the way back to when I was twelve years old. I remembered going to church and seeing Josh, how our stories were different whenever we would meet. I used to talk about hanging out, fighting, smoking weed, doing cocaine, and stealing cars. He talked about school, homework, and the extracurricular activities that followed his school day. The difference in his lifestyle and choices and mine was stark. I was proud of him, and a part of me wished I had chosen the same course he had.

Josh's situation was a little different from my own though. Throughout my prison bid there was one thing that stayed on my brain consistently. At my trial, my lawyer had said that if I had grown up in a different environment, I would never have been exposed to or been a part of the crimes I was convicted of then. My mother had moved to the projects when I was ten years old. Josh and his parents had moved to more affluent neighborhoods. Therein lay a major disparity. It was after my release party that I realized that I should try to help others who may not have had the same opportunities as those more fortunate. It was in my heart to try to help others like me not to become a part of the prison culture.

If I could speak to those young men, maybe I could make a difference, maybe I could show them something that they otherwise would not ever see or hear if not for me showing up and saying it. I had many goals I wanted to achieve now that I was out, and now one of them was public speaking and mentoring. I was in my early twenties, and there were plenty young men that needed to hear my story.

I continued my job at the bakery even after I was released. I had some money saved from my stay at the halfway house, and I was anxious to spend it. I immediately bought a Cadillac and put rims on it, very reminiscent of the cars that I was so infatuated with before my incarceration. I bought a whole new wardrobe, clothing and shoes. I was young and fresh out of prison; I had a lot of catching up to do, and I dove in head first.

Atlanta had changed drastically in the ten years that I was gone. The hip-hop music scene was livelier now in Atlanta than it had ever been. People from all over the country would end up in Atlanta on any given weekend to enjoy the music hub. The nightclubs were infamous, and excessively flaunting one's means of wealth was the "in" thing. Popping bottles of champagne, wearing designer clothing and jewelry were all staples of enjoying the nightlife. I had been gone for so many years that it was easy for me to get caught up in the melee. I found myself hanging out at the clubs two or three nights of the week. Quickly, my savings began to diminish.

I eventually quit my job even before I found a new job. It was then that I got the rude awakening; nobody was looking to hire a convicted felon. My probation officer was concerned about my lack of employment since it was required for me to stay employed during my probation. She told me she could assist me with a part-time job as a motivational speaker. It didn't pay much, yet I would be able to speak to young people and share my story plus make enough money to put gas in my car while I searched for a job.

I had depleted my savings with my new lifestyle, and I couldn't find a job. A desire to get money fast was swelling in my chest, and I knew that there was one way that I could make money and fast. I had sworn to my family, friends, and even myself that I would never resort back to hustling, but that old feeling was crouching at the base of my skull.

Just as I was about to venture into the realms of the street life again, I was hired as a truck driver, but not just any truck driver, I was delivering portable toilets from one place to another and pumping the waste from them. Though the pay was better, I still found the job to be humiliating and depressing.

At night, before bed, no matter how many showers I took or how hard I scrubbed, I could not get rid of the putrid smell that began to live in my flesh. I was determined to do better, but being a convicted felon was a strong deterrent.

While in the portable toilet business, I worked alongside a young man named Jose. Jose was a Mexican, and he didn't have any complaints about the job or its duties. I assumed that it was because of his nationality that he was content. One day, in the break room, I had a conversation with him.

"How do you deal with this shit, Jose?" I asked, I really needed to be enlightened.

Most everyone else I had worked with felt the same way I did, and without words you could detect their disdain just by their facial expressions.

Jose was different, though. He smiled and shrugged his shoulders.

"I don't have to be here, holmes," he replied coyly. "I work because the white man says I have too. I don't need no heat on me."

I listened to Jose intently. I was trying to catch his angle. I knew what he was hinting at by his use of the word "heat", but I was skeptical about coming out and saying it. My curiosity eventually won.

"So, what you do, bro? You got a side hustle? You on parole?" I asked covertly as I leaned in closely.

He nodded. "Mota," he said bluntly.

"What is that?" I asked.

He laughed. "Let's go outside," he said. "I need a cigarette."

It was outside, in front of the port-a-pot warehouse, that Jose told me about the marijuana business. Then he offered me a job. The agreement was that he would give me pounds of weed up front and I would pay him from what I sold. Consignment, the weed, would pay for itself. By the time Jose had finished his cigarette, I had signed on to pick up my first pound of weed.

From that day forward, I was back in business. I had been out of prison for two years, and the memories of that stay seemed distant. I was in a much different place now, and the initial fear of returning to prison that I had when I first got out was absent. So I dove in the weed game head first.

Selling weed was not a violent hustle. It was easy, and the money was consistent. I didn't have the same strategy as Jose though. After two months, I quit the job and went into selling weed full time. I bought a Jaguar and put rims on it. I was finally making enough money to live the lifestyle I desired. I frequented all the happening nightclubs; if there was a party, I was there too. I felt like I was owed a good time. After all the hardships I had endured over the years, it felt good to be content and free.

As time passed, so did my focus. I never forgot the prison experience, but how often I thought about it had changed. The memories of prison and its hardship became blotted out by alcohol, marijuana, music, and women. All the things I had daydreamed about while I was locked away, I was living them now and in premiere fashion.

124

I was an adult. I knew exactly what I was doing and how I wanted to accomplish things. I wasn't hiding from my mother or relatives. I had my own place and was living my own life. I wasn't endangering the lives of others or my own. I had a great relationship with my mother, and even my father and I had gotten closer. More importantly, I wasn't reduced to pumping shit from a toilet. In the workforce, I was a convicted felon. With the weed hustle, I was a businessman.

Before tragedy strikes, there are always warning signs. My warning came in the form of a meeting with my father. We met at a Waffle House downtown. We embraced in the parking lot and headed inside. We sat at a booth and ordered. I had been communicating with my dad over the phone on a regular basis since I was released, but seeing him face to face happened only once a year. I was surprised when he called and told me he was in the city. In the booth, we talked about the family, his job, and sports until the food came.

After our plates arrived, his face turned serious. "You know I've been trying to get back acquainted with the church," he began. "I'm definitely not here to preach to you, but I came across a passage in the Bible that made me think about you."

I cut into a slither of steak. "What you got?" I asked, genuinely interested.

He put two sugar packets into his coffee and stirred before he spoke. "In the book of Matthew, chapter twenty-five, there is a story of a master who gave his servants talents, which was money at this particular time. But I want you to consider these as actual talents, like your football skills."

I listened a little more intently.

"Two of the servants each took their talents and doubled them. The third servant simply buried his talent. The one who buried his talent thought that he had done the right thing, but, in the end, the master found favor in the servants who had utilized their talents and the master made them more than what they were before."

I was listening, waiting for the explanation, but that was all he said. I didn't pry any further because I felt that he wanted me to come to my own conclusions. We carried on with breakfast as if that bit of information had never been spoken. I understood what he meant, and I reflected on that jewel the rest of the day. I knew that I could put more efforts into manifesting my true talents, and I even vowed that evening that I would make changes in my life. I had even put it in my mind to read Matthew, chapter twenty-five. By the next morning, though, it was back to life as I knew it. My current talent was selling weed.

A few nights after the breakfast meeting with my father, a few friends and I were on our way to Club 112. 112 was a trendy nightclub in the upscale part of the city. Anybody who was successful—athletes, entertainers, and other celebrities—patronized the establishment. Money had been good for me that week, and I was looking forward to blowing some of it in the club that evening.

That night, two of my friends and I were drinking Hennessy and blowing some of the best marijuana known to man in the Jaguar on our way to Club 112. Life was the best it had ever been for me in that exact moment. Not everyone could do what I was doing, and I knew it. I was truly content with my life. But that was short-lived. I saw blue lights in my rearview mirror, and my heart sank to my sneakers. It was the police.

The invincible mindset that I had been in for the last eight months vanished like vapor. It felt just like when waking up from sleep, after a great dream. This was no dream. As I pulled the car over, I understood that I would be going to jail. It was just that simple. We had weed in the car, the car smelled like weed, and I had been drinking. What had started out as a normal day in the life of Kenyatta had taken an unprecedented turn for the worse. The car reeked of marijuana, and it only took a second for the cop to smell it. We were all taken out of the car so that they could search the vehicle, and that search turned up more marijuana and some open containers of alcohol.

Once again, I was handcuffed and put into the back of a police cruiser. I was sweating, I knew that my worst fear had come to pass. There was less than an ounce of weed in the car, and the open container ticket for the alcohol would be nothing more than a citation. Still, I knew that I wouldn't be getting a slap on the hand. I was a convicted felon, and I was still on probation.

The holding tank, the county jail, the courtroom. The revocation of the remainder of my probation, the handcuffs, and the leg shackles. The early morning bus ride to prison, serving time. These were all things that I had experienced before. It was a way of life now. I was officially a career criminal. I had eighteen months left on my probation, and the judge wanted me to serve the rest of it in a minimum-security prison. I knew that I would be out again, sooner rather than later. I knew that I would forever be a convicted felon. I also understood that, no matter what, I would at the very least forever have control over my decision-making process. I vowed then to make better decisions.

The minimum-security prison where I was sent to finish my eighteen months was not as imposing as Alto had been. There weren't as many barbed wire fences here, the food was better, and the inmate-on-inmate violence was almost nonexistent. We were all going home soon. We even played flag football sometimes. I was still young and exceptional on the field.

One day, I walked off the field and over to the water keg. A correctional officer was standing nearby as I filled my paper cup.

"Kenyatta," he said, "you're pretty good out there on that field, son. What are you going to do with all that talent?"